POLITICS AND ECONOMICS OF JAPAN: AN ANNOTATED BIBLIOGRAPHY

Edited by W.D. Alema

Nova Science Publishers, Inc.

Politics and Economics of Japan: An Annotated Bibliography

Politics and Economics of Japan: An Annotated Bibliography

Edited by: W.D. Alema

Nova Science Publishers, Inc.

Nova Science Publishers, Inc.
6080 Jericho Turnpike, Suite 207
Commack, New York 11725

Electronic Book Production Manager:
Denise Engelhardt
Graphics: Elenor Kallberg, Christopher Concannon,
and Michael A. Masotti
Cover Design: Christopher Concannon

Library of Congress Cataloging-in-Publication Data available upon request

ISBN 1-56072-049-2

Printed in the United States of America

CONTENTS

PREFACE

This compilation represents an attempt to gather descriptive citations concerning the economics and politics of Japan. The materials presented here form the beginning of a project to regularly publish descriptive citations and lists of articles dealing with this important theme. We have attempted to group the entries in what is hoped will be a logical format and augmented them with subject and author indexes for multiple access points

W.D. Alema June 1992

A. DOMESTIC POLITICS; FOREIGN POLICY; ECONOMIC POLICY

A001. **ANALYSIS OF THE U.S.-JAPAN TRADE PROBLEM; REPORT.** [Washington]: The Committee, 1989, 122 pp.

Analyzes the U.S.-Japan trade relationship, assesses the successes and failures of past negotiating efforts, and offers a series of recommendations that the ACTPN hopes will produce meaningful results without unnecessary straining the relationship. Concludes that any solution to trade problems must also consider changes in fiscal and monetary policies as well as changes in trade practices.

A002. Anderson, S.J. **THE POLITICAL ECONOMY OF JAPANESE SAVING: HOW POSTAL SAVINGS AND PUBLIC PENSIONS SUPPORT HIGH RATES OF HOUSEHOLD SAVING IN JAPAN.** *Journal of Japanese Studies*, Vol. 16, Winter 1990, pp. 61–92.

Demonstrates policy priorities in Japan directly support increased savings and that government activities toward public pensions and postal savings result in continuing high levels of household saving.

A003. **THE ANGRY SUN: THE MAKING OF A JAPANESE REVISIONIST.** *Tokyo Business Today*, Vol. 57, Dec 1989, pp. 22–25.

The LDP's Ishihara Shintaro, together with Sony's Morita Akio, has written a Japanese revisionist view of America titled *A Japan That Can Say 'No.'* This essay provoked a sensation in Washington.

A004. Arnold, W. **POLITICAL AND ECONOMIC INFLUENCES IN JAPAN'S RELATIONS WITH CHINA SINCE 1978.** *Millenium*, Vol. 18, Winter 1989, pp. 415–434.

This article analyses Sino-Japanese relations largely from a dependency perspective. It attempts to determine the extent to which political factors have influenced Sino-Japanese economic relations by applying Albert O. Hirschman's theory of the economic influence effect to Sino-Japanese trade, investment and foreign aid.

A005. Atsushi, O. **KAIFU TOSHIKI: PRIME MINISTER BETWIXT AND BETWEEN.** *Japan Quarterly*, Vol. 36, Oct–Dec 1989, pp. 368–374.

Aug. 9, 1989, when Kaifu Toshiki Cabinet came into being, will be remembered for the ripple it made in the chronicles of modern Japanese politics.

A006. Baerwald, H.H. **JAPAN'S 39th HOUSE OF REPRESENTATIVES ELECTION: A CASE OF MIXED SIGNALS.** *Asian Survey*, Vol. 30, June 1990, pp. 541–559.

An oxymoron for Japan's long-governing Liberal Democratic Party? Voters to the polls twice in eight months and overturn their earlier verdict in the second election. This article will explore some of the factors that might explain these reversals of voter preferences.

A007. Baerwald, H.H. **JAPAN'S HOUSE OF COUNCILORS ELECTION: A MINI-REVOLUTION?** *Asian Survey*, Vol. 29, Sept. 1989, pp. 833–841.

The long-governing Liberal Democratic Party (LDP) in Japan lost a national election for the first time since it was organized in the Fall of 1955....The long-declining Japan Socialist Party (JSP) enjoyed the sweet taste of victory under the leadership of Takako Doi, the first woman to head one of Japan's major political parties.

A008. Bernstein, G.L. **JAPANESE MARXIST: A PORTRAIT OF KAWAKAMI HAJIME, 1879–1946.** Harvard Univ. Pr., 1990, ISBN 0-674-47194-6.

A009. Bloch, J.C. **A U.S.-JAPAN AID ALLIANCE: PROSPECTS FOR COOPERATION IN AN ERA OF CONFLICT.** Cambridge: Program on U.S.-Japan Relations, Harvard Univ., 1989, 18 pp.

Contents.—Origins and evolution: an historical perspective of development aid.—Philosophies and purposes: Creating markets or buying allies.—Players and politics: policymaking in aid systems.—Changing roles and responsibilities: accommodating today's economic realities.—Cooperation or conflict: Prospects for a U.S.-Japan aid alliance.

A010. Bobrow, D.B. and Kudrle, R.T. **U.S. POLICY AND JAPAN: BEYOND SELF-INDULGENCE.** *Comparative Strategy*, Vol. 9, No. 2, 1990, pp. 101–115.

Bilateral relations between the United States and Japan now rival with the Soviet Union in overall importance. Unfortunately, the United States has engaged in self-indulgence by blaming Japan for a variety of ills, many of which reflect U.S. weaknesses.

A011. Bridges, B. **JAPAN: BUSINESS AS USUAL?** *World Today*, Vol. 46, Apr 1990, pp. 58–61.

Major reversals in the political power structure of Japan has been forecast several times over the past two decades, but they have never materialized....For all their disillusionment with the LDP only a few months earlier, the Japanese voters in the February election seemed to be swayed by the maxim of 'better the devil you know.'

A012. Bronfenbrenner, M. **THE JAPANESE POLITICAL ECONOMY: AN EXPATRIOTS POINT OF VIEW.** *World and I*, Vol. 5, May 1990, pp. 575–587.

Focuses on the differences between the Japanese and U.S. economies, claiming that much of Japan's economy is organized and regulated corporatively under the aegis of publicly supervised trade or industrial associations. Offers a variety of response to the Japanese challenges, favoring a revision of our own politico-economic system, insofar as it works badly. This approach entails leaving the Japanese alone rather than forcing them to change their system against their will.

A013. Brooks, R.A. and Brick, A.B. **BUSH'S TRIP TO TOKYO, BEIJING, AND SEOUL, FEBRUARY 24–27, 1989: REAFFIRMING AMERICA'S SPECIAL ROLE IN ASIA.** Washington: Heritage Foundation, 1989, 9 pp.

George Bush's first international trip as president. He will also be dealing with the important challenges in trade, defense, and diplomacy that the United States faces in Asia. Outlines recommendations for Bush as he meets with leaders in Tokyo, Beijing, and Seoul.

A014. Brown, H. **THE UNITED STATES AND JAPAN: HIGH TECH IS FOREIGN POLICY.** *SAIS Review*, Vol. 9, Summer–Fall 1989, pp. 1–18.

The increased impact of economic and technological factors on international security requires a closer look at the U.S.-Japanese partnership, especially as Japan equals, and might soon surpass, the United States in technological capability.

A015. Buruma, I. **AFTER HIROHITO: WHAT REMAINS SACRED (THE REVIVAL OF IMPERIAL MYTHS COULD BE DANGEROUS FOR JAPAN).** *New York Times Magazine*, Sec. 6, May 28, 1989, pp. 28–29, 52, 54, 59, 64.

Japan may be enjoying unprecedented economic success, but partly as a result, it is deeply uncertain about its relations with the outside world and about where the nation is heading. The attempt to revive native values in Japan, as in other countries, is usually a sign of crisis.

A016. Calder, K.E. **ELITES IN AN EQUALIZING ROLE: EX-BUREAUCRATS AS COORDINATORS AND INTERMEDIARIES IN THE JAPANESE GOVERNMENT-BUSINESS RELATIONSHIP.** *Comparative Politics*, Vol. 21, July 1989, pp. 379–403.

Over the past half century, the steady expansion of government services and regulatory powers throughout the world has sharply increased the level of interdependence between private groups and state authority....Japan clearly is a nation in which government power and administrative activities are at present deeply intertwined with those of the private sector, making it difficult to discuss public policy abstracted from private interest.

A017. **THE CENTRAL BANKS VS. THE POLITICIANS.** *International Economy*, Vol. 4, June–July 1990, pp. 60–69.

Contents.—Washington: the Fed has the edge on the economic policy front, by Tom Redburn.—Tokyo: is monetary policy still out of sync at the top, by Bill Chapman.—Bonn: the Bundesbank loses some of its luster, by Klaus Engelen.

A018. Choate, P. **POLITICAL ADVANTAGE: JAPAN'S CAMPAIGN FOR AMERICA.** *Harvard Business Review*, Vol. 68, Sept.–Oct. 1990, pp. 87–103.

Claims that the most successful political economic machine in the United States belongs to the Japanese. Each year, Japanese companies and the Japanese government invest $400 million in an ongoing campaign that is designed to keep the U.S. market open or Japanese exports....to influence U.S. trade policies toward Japan and Europe, and to create an integrated U.S.–Japan economy that prevents the United States from confronting Japan. Asserts that the campaign operates at five levels: intelligence gathering, lobbying and influencing policy, politicking at the grass roots level, dispersing propaganda, and influencing U.S. education and classroom instruction.

A019. Cox, R.W. **MIDDLEPOWERMANSHIP, JAPAN, AND FUTURE WORLD ORDER.** *International Journal*, Vol. 44, Autumn 1989, pp. 823–862.

The author attempts to explore the middle-power role in the changing international system by taking up three questions: (1) What is the essence of the middle power's functional relationship to world order? (2) What are the key elements in the current problem of world order and....(3) What are Japan's options and the prospects of it performing the middle-power function?

A020. Dillon, K.J. **WORLDS IN COLLUSION: THE US AND JAPAN BEYOND THE YEAR 2000**. Washington: Center for the Study of Foreign Affairs, 1989, 27 pp.

Claims that four scenarios for U.S.-Japan relations seem possible in the future: 1) Japan eclipses the US; 2) the US and Japan cooperate as equals in leading the world to new heights of prosperity; 3) a resurgent US overshadows Japan; and 4) bitter quarreling causes an entranged US and Japan to retreat into their own blocs. Of these, Scenario 2 (with a dash of Scenario 4) appears most likely.

A021. Dratler, J. Jr. **TRADE SECRETS IN THE UNITED STATES AND JAPAN: A COMPARISON AND PROGNOSIS.** *Yale Journal of International Law*, Vol. 14, Winter 1989, pp. 68–117.

Article compares trade secret protection in the U.S. and Japan with emphasis on cultural and political factors that underlie weak protection measures in Japan.

A022. Drifte, R. **JAPAN'S RISE TO INTERNATIONAL RESPONSIBILITIES: THE CASE OF ARMS CONTROL.** Atlantic Highlands: Athlone Press, 1990, 112 pp.

Includes bibliographic references. Arms control. Japan—Military relations.

A023. Farnsworth, L.W. **CLAN POLITICS AND JAPAN'S CHANGING POLICY-MAKING STRUCTURE.** *World Economy*, Vol. 12, June 1989, pp. 163–174.

Examines the structure of and the exertion of influence by groups of Japanese Diet members known as "zoku giin" or "coordinators of policy." Answers the questions: What do zoku giin do? What are their personal and carrier attributes? What kind of vertical hierarchy exists them? What kind of horizontal specialization is there?

A024. Fisher, R.D. Jr. **HOW TO IMPROVE THE U.S.-JAPAN SECURITY ALLIANCE**. Washington: Heritage Foundation, Asian Studies Center, 1990, 15 pp.

The United States-Japan military alliance is being strained. Declining Cold-War tensions between the U.S. and the Soviet Union and rising economic competition between the U.S. and Japan are placing unprecedented pressures on it....This alliance is the basis for long-term stability in Asia and the linchpin of American strategy in Asia.

A025. **FOCUS ON FOREIGN AID.** *Japan Echo*, Vol. 16, Spring 1989, pp. 6–28.

Contents—Directing Japan's aid efforts, by Yanagiya Kensuke and Yamaguchi Mitsuhide. Problems in the aid program, by Mera Koichi. Foreign aid: a dissenter's view, by A. Motoo. Handling the influx of foreign workers, by S. Haruo.

A026. **FORUM: JAPAN–U.S. RELATIONS.** *Congressional Research Service Review*, Vol. 10, July 1989, pp. 1–23.

Contents—A more open Japanese market?, by R.A. Ahearn. Japan–U.S. trade: looking ahead, by W.H. Cooper. Technology policy in Japan and the Unites States, by G.J. McLoughlin. Japanese investment in the United States, by J.K. Jackson. Japan's emergence as a leading foreign aid donor, by L.K. Nowels. Japan's expanding economic role and influence in Asia, by R.P. Cronin. Burden sharing and power sharing, by L.A. Niksch. Japan and an East Asian trading bloc, by D.K. Nanto.

A027. Fukunaga, H. **THE LDP AND PRIME MINISTER UNO: NOWHERE TO TURN.** *Tokyo Business Today*, July 1989, pp. 14–19.

The Recruit scandal revealed the extent of influence peddling in Japanese politics. With the selection of Sousuke Uno as prime minister, the LDP has attempted to put the scandal behind it. But there are rumors that his administration won't last long, strengthening the role of Takeshita as a behind-the-scenes power broker.

A028. **FY 1990 OUTLOOK FOR THE JAPANESE ECONOMY.** Washington: Japanese Economic Institute, 1990, 15 pp.

More than three years after the Japanese economy touched bottom in late 1986, its forward progress seems unstoppable. For fiscal 1989, which ends March 31, price-adjusted gross national product is nearly certain to grow more than 4 percent and perhaps as much as 5 percent. Most Japanese analysts expect growth to be almost as high in fiscal 1990, absent any special factors.

A029. Giscard d'Estaing, V., Nakasone, Y. and Kissinger, H.A. **EAST–WEST RELATIONS.** *Foreign Affairs*, Vol. 68, Summer 1989, pp. 1–21.

"East–West relations have entered a new phase. Changes in the Soviet Union's domestic and foreign policies have already affected the climate of East–West relations and, in some areas, its substance....We have prepared this report in the belief that our countries face a challenge that will shape the future of international relations for several decades. So far, our countries have not reached a consensus on the significance of this challenge, on the degree to which it reflects a lasting change in Soviet policies, or even on our own attitudes in relation to it."

A030. Grimm, M. **TRILATERAL TIES: JAPAN THE UNITED STATES AND THE PHILIPPINES.** Washington: Japan Economic Institute, 1990, 19 pp.

Discusses the trilateral relationship of the U.S., Japan, and the Philippines given the decreased Soviet threat and the aid needs of the new democracies in Eastern Europe. Asserts that despite these changes, the enormity of the Philippine's problems, ranging from heavy foreign debt and political instability to poverty and hunger, demand particular attention from Japan and the United States.

A031. Gross, N. **CHARGING JAPAN WITH CRIMES AGAINST THE EARTH.** *Business Week*, No. 3127, Oct. 9, 1989, 108, p. 112.

At home, Japan has cleaned up its environment. But abroad, the Japanese continue to earn international ire. Its companies have failed to curb industrial pollution overseas. And Japan continues to support environmentally destructive aid projects....But those actions don't come close to placating critics.

A032. Gross, N. and Borrus, A. **JAPAN: WILL THE RECRUIT SCANDAL JUST GO AWAY?** *Business Week*, No. 3109, June 12, 1989, pp. 40–41.

Examines events in Japan, as that country's Liberal Democratic Party, selects a new Prime Minister in the wake of the Recruit scandal.

A033. **GUILTY AS CHARGED?** *Business Tokyo*, Vol. 4, Nov. 1990, pp. 18–24.

Critiques Pat Choate's recent publication (Agents of Influence) which accuses the Japanese government and industry of waging an unceasing, well-orchestrated and expensive campaign to purchase influence in America.

A034. Gyohten, T. **SUPPORT FOR LATIN AMERICA: A QUALIFIED PROMISE.** *Speaking of Japan*, Vol. 11, June 1990, pp. 22–24.

Toyoo Cyohten, special advisor to the Finance Minister of Japan, presents his views on the Latin American debt crisis.

A035. Haber, D.L. **THE DEATH OF HEGEMONY: WHY "PAX NIPPONICA" IS IMPOSSIBLE.** *Asian Survey*, Vol. 30, Sept. 1990, pp. 892–907.

The notion of hegemony will be explored and two different definitions of hegemony provided as a framework for demonstrating that Japan does not have the capacity to dominate world politics or economics. The two definitions of hegemony applied to Japan's relations with China and India to illustrate the limitations on Japan's ability to dominate Asia.

A036. Hanami, T. (Ed.) **INDUSTRIAL CONFLICT RESOLUTION IN MARKET ECONOMIES STUDY OF AUSTRALIA, FEDERAL REPUBLIC OF GERMANY, ITALY, JAPAN, AND THE USA**, 2nd edition. Kluwer Academic Pub., 1989, ISBN 9-06-544418-1, 342 pp.

A037. Helleiner, E. **MONEY AND INFLUENCE: JAPANESE POWER IN THE INTERNATIONAL MONETARY AND FINANCIAL SYSTEM.** *Millennium*, Vol. 18, Winter 1989, pp. 343–358.

Examines the growing power of Japan in the international financial system, concentrating on two separate developments: Japan's emergence as a creditor nation and the internationalization of the Japanese financial system. Each of these can be seen to have brought a different kind of power to the Japanese state.

A038. Higashi, C. **INTERNATIONALIZATION OF THE JAPANESE ECONOMY.** 2nd Ed. Kluwer Academic Pub., 1990, ISBN 0-7923-9052-0.

A039. Hisae, S. **THE POLITICAL AWAKENING OF WOMEN.** *Japan Quarterly*, Vol. 36, Oct.–Dec. 1989, pp. 381–385.

Examines the increasing participation of women in Japanese politics.

A040. Holstein, W.J. **THE JAPANESE POWER GAME: WHAT IT MEANS FOR AMERICA.** New York: Charles Scribner's Sons, 1990, 339 pp.

In a series of revelations, Holstein shows how hopes for political and social change in Japan in the wake of the Recruit scandal were dramatically overblown. It was the challengers to the status quo, not the establishment, who were punished. Nor have the Japanese lost their competitive clout. Even as the Japanese power game is played at home, the Japanese are extending their systems and values to the United States and increasing their influence on American perceptions and politics.

A041. Horne, M.K. **THE NORTHERN TERRITORIES: SOURCE OR SYMPTOM?** *Journal of Northeast Asian Studies,* Vol. 8, Winter 1989, pp. 60–76.

The issue of the Northern Territories has often been described as the 'centerpiece' of Soviet–Japanese relations, and this is seemingly reflected in the forty-five years of postwar diplomatic history between the Soviet Union and Japan....This article suggests that the islands dispute is a symptom, not a source, of the tension that has been generated by the timing and course of modernization taken by these two neighbors.

A042. Horvat, A. **WHERE THE COLD WAR IS COLDEST.** *International Economy,* Vol. 4, Feb.–Mar. 1990, pp. 66–69.

With Soviet–Japanese relations stalemated over the 'Northern Territories,' Japan can maintain a status quo of cool relations with the Soviets and a military dependence on the U.S. by means of the U.S.–Japan security treaty.

A043. Ikle, F.C. and Nakanishi, T. **JAPAN'S GRAND STRATEGY.** *Foreign Affairs,* Vol. 69, Summer 1990, pp. 81–95.

The time has come for Japan to develop a sense of purpose for contributing to a peaceful world on a scope commensurate with its enormous economic and technological strength. Japan needs a grand strategy consonant with its elf-image as a humanistic, democratic and peaceful nation, and a strategy able to win broad support among the Japanese people. To this end, the geographic horizon of Japan's defense policy must expand beyond the region of the Japanese islands.

A044. Inada, J. **JAPAN'S AID DIPLOMACY: ECONOMIC, POLITICAL OR STRATEGIC?** *Millennium,* Vol. 18, Winter 1989, pp. 399–414.

Intention to shed some light on the actual state of Japan's aid program....considers three questions in the Japanese context: (1) is aid becoming more political, or 'strategic,' in nature? (2) What political and diplomatic considerations go into the formation of aid diplomacy? (3) Is aid still dominated by commercial interests?

A046. **THE INTERNATIONAL RELATIONS OF JAPAN.** *Millennium,* Vol. 18, Winter 1989, whole issue pp. 329–478.

Contents—Money and influence: Japanese power in the international monetary and financial system, by E. Helleiner. The Japanese industrial presence in America: same, bed, different dreams, by Michael Hodges. The Third World in Japanese foreign policy, by W. Nester. Japan's aid diplomacy: economic, political, or strategic? by J. Inada. Political and economic influences in Japan's relations with China since 1978, by W. Arnold.

Japan's security policy after U.S. hegemony, by T. Akaha. Stuck in a mold: the relationship between Japan and Soviet Union, by W. Mendl.

A047. Ishihara, S. **PLAYBOY INTERVIEW: SHINTARO ISHIHARA.** *Playboy,* Vol. 37, Oct. 1990, pp. 59–60,63,65–66,68,70,76,84.

In a candid interview with the coauthor of the Japan That Can Say No, discusses Japanese economic power and the changing relationship with the U.S.

A048. Ishihara, S. **SHINTARO ISHIHARA: ADVICE FOR AN AILING GIANT.** *International Economy,* Vol. 4, Oct.–Nov. 1990, pp. 65–69.

Japan's leading U.S. critic offers advice—and some additional criticism—aimed at U.S. politicians.

A049. Ishikawa, K. **JAPAN AND THE CHALLENGE OF EUROPE 1992.** London: Pinter Publishers, 1990, 151 pp.

The real arguments [over 1992] have only just begun and any battle over such matters promises to be especially difficult and hard fought,' says Kenjiro Ishikawa, who perceptively analyses the possible outcomes of the changes that the 1992 program for the creation of a single European market may bring about in the relationship between Japan and Europe. Drawing on an impressively wide range of data, the author carefully examines the agenda for adjustment.

A050. Islam, S. **CAPITALISM IN CONFLICT.** *Foreign Affairs,* Vol. 69, No. 1, 1990, pp. 172–182.

Asserts that future historians may choose 1989 as the year the cold war between capitalism and communism ended and a new conflict began within capitalism. They may argue that it was in 1989 that America and the West turned from containing the Soviet Union to containing Japan. The new conflict arises from three historic shifts that have shaken the foundations of the postwar world: America's relative economic decline, the rising economic power of Japan, and the decline of the West's old common enemy of communism.

A051. Islam, S. (Ed.) **YEN FOR DEVELOPMENT: JAPANESE FOREIGN AID & THE POLITICS OF BURDEN-SHARING.** New York: Council on Foreign Relations, 1991, ISBN 0-87609-096-X, 265 pp.

In this ground-breaking volume, a group of Japanese and American aid experts, academics and officials from both countries and multilateral development institutions convened by the Council on Foreign Relations explores the new, and sometimes surprising, impact of Japan on international development and on the bilateral politics of foreign aid.

A052. Jain, P. **UNDER THE BAMBOO: SOME CHARACTERISTICS OF JAPANESE POLITICS.** *Asian Thought and Society,* Vol. 15, Jan. 1990, pp. 17–32.

The purpose of this short article is not to assess the successes or failures of the Takeshita administration. On the contrary, the main aim is to highlight a few characteristics of Japanese politics which became more visible during his administration.

A053. **JAPAN 1990.** *Far Eastern Economic Review*, Vol. 148, June 21, 1990, pp. 37,39–40,42,44–45,47–48,50,54,56,58,60–63,65–66.

Addresses the challenges facing Japan in the foreign policy arena as well as in the domestic economy. In a series of articles, claims that Japan's affluent workaholics may have to adapt to Western-style consumerism. Other changes could include drastic modifications of a number of traditional institutions such as the way Japan's bureaucracy works. Another candidate for treatment could be the keiretsu system of industrial groupings which have served Japan's economic interests superbly in the past but are definitely not serving to promote access to the economy by foreigners.

A054. **JAPAN'S AMERICA—BASHERS: AMERICA'S ASSERTIVE ALLIES.** *Orbis*, Vol. 34, Winter 1990, pp. 83–102.

While both sides consider the relationship between them vital, neither believes that it can continue on its present course. It is in this context that Akio Morita and Shintaro Ishihara wrote the Japan That Can Say No: The New U.S.–Japan Relations Card....In it, two very different Japanese notables express their frustrations with U.S.–Japan relations. Ishihara is a nationalist and a politician; Morita is an internationalist and a businessman....Toward this end, the following pages provide a report on the contents of the manuscript. Contents—The background, by Andrew Goble. Editor's note. The manuscripts, by J.C. Carlson.

A055. **JAPAN AND THE PROBLEM OF KAMPUCHEA.** *Contemporary Southeast Asia*, Vol. 11, Dec. 1989, pp. 313–331.

On its own, Kampuchea would not have been of importance to Japan. Yet, given the international political alignment pattern in the late 1970s, it had to give some attention to the problem of Kampuchea. With growing Soviet–Vietnamese relations and the invasion of Kampuchea, Japan leaned to the side of ASEAN and China. Japan's attempts to play a mediatory role between the conflicting parties have not been successful. Thus, for the time being, Japan is prepared to allow ASEAN to take the initiative.

A056. **JAPAN AND THE UNITED STATES.** *Japan Echo*, Vol. 16, Summer 1989, pp. 58–74.

Contents—U.S. pressure: boon or bane?, by K. Atsushi. Japan as number two, by N. Terumasa. Making Japan a better partner, by T. Jitsuro.

A057. **THE JAPANESE MONARCHY.** *Japan Echo*, Vol. 16, Summer 1989, pp. 6–27.

Contents—The imperial institution: Japan's unbroken thread, by M. Shumon, and Y. Shichiehi. The Showa emperor and his era, by Y. Masakazu, and K. Masataka. Defending the dignity of the symbolic emperor, by N. Susumu.

A058. Johnson, B.T. **JAPANESE FOREIGN AID: DEFINING AMERICA'S INTERESTS.** Washington, Heritage Foundation, 1990, 11 pp.

The poor of the world will be losers if Tokyo and Washington use foreign assistance funds to battle one another for export markets. History demonstrates that the best means by which a poor country can develop—as the new governments in Eastern Europe reaffirm—is though a free market economy. America, therefore, instead of competing with Japan's aid program, should work with the Japanese to construct programs that promote market-oriented economic growth and sound economic policies in less developed countries.

A059. Johnson, U.A., Okawara, Y., Goodpaster, A.J., Saeki, K., Volcker, P.A. and Hosomi, T. **THE UNITED STATES AND JAPAN: COOPERATIVE LEADERSHIP FOR PEACE AND GLOBAL PROSPERITY.** Lanham: University Press of America, ISBN 0-8191-7712-1, 126 pp.

Increased opportunities for political and economic cooperation between the United States and Japan led to the initiation of this bilateral policy planning report. A Committee of Six, co-chaired by Ambassador U. Alexis Johnson and Ambassador Yoshio Okawara, and including General Andrew J. Goodpaster, Takashi Hosomi, Kiichi Saeki and Paul A. Volcker, commissioned research on economic and politico-security relations and conducted extensive consultations with a wide range of U.S. and Japanese policy-makers and private sector leaders. The principle conclusion is that a worldwide process of economic integration has established an interdependent relationship between the U.S. economy, the Japanese economy, and the world economy: Neither Japan nor the United States alone can continue to prosper unless both prosper, and unless economic growth is widely shared and sustained in the developing world as well.

A060. Jones, L.R. and Thompson, F. **BURDEN SHARING AMONG AMERICA AND ITS ALLIES: TESTS OF COLLECTIVE CHOICE AND THEIR SIGNIFICANCE.** *Western Political Quarterly*, Vol. 43, Sept. 1990, pp. 459–477.

Explains how application of the free rider thesis to the problem of collective security can be revised in the light of contemporary thinking about the provision of collective goods; presents some preliminary tests of this formulation; and suggests a few of the implications of this analysis for the formulation of United States defense policy.

A061. Judis, J.B. **THE JAPANESE MEGAPHONE.** *New Republic*, Vol. 202, Jan. 22, 1990, pp. 20–25.

Describes the supposed structural corruption that Japanese government agencies, corporations, and foundations are creating in the United States through their funding of think tanks, Japanese studies programs, and lobbyists, consultants and public relations advisers. The hundreds of millions that Japan is spending annually are tilting the debate about America's economic future without the public being aware of it. The Japanese are radically reinforcing options that mirror their own....It's hard for Americans to have a meaningful debate when Japan and its lobbyists have acquired such extensive influence over the debate itself.

A062. Judis, J.B. **A YEN FOR APPROVAL.** *Columbia Journalism Review*, Vol. 28, Jan. 1990 pp. 42–45.

Looks at Japan's recent spending on lobbying efforts in the U.S. Japan's massive investment in American opinion has raised a host of questions about press coverage. Japanese firms, foundations, and government agencies have funded American television and radio shows on U.S.–Japan relations. Should U.S. television and radio accept this kind of funding?

A063. Kades, C.L. **THE AMERICAN ROLE IN REVISING JAPAN'S IMPERIAL CONSTITUTION.** *Political Science Quarterly*, Vol. 104, Summer 1989, pp. 215–247.

The author from the perspective of a participant observer, tells the story of the drafting and enacting process after World War II of Japan's current constitution. He suggests that the constitution was not simply imposed but resulted from a joint enterprise of two former enemies working together.

A064. Kasindorf, M. **REAGAN'S FALL FROM GRACE.** *Los Angeles Times Magazine*, Mar. 4, 1990, pp. 10–16,18–19.

The $2-million Japan tour, Nancy's vengeful memoirs (My Turn) and legal battles over the Iran-Contra affair have made his retirement anything but restful. Discusses former President Reagan's serious problem of public perception, especially focusing on the economic aspects of his retirement.

A065. Kaufmann, S.-Y. **POLITICAL ROLE OF JAPAN IN WORLD AFFAIRS.** *Korea and World Affairs*, Vol. 13, Spring 1990, pp.16–33.

The current debates on Japan's foreign and security policies indicate that policy-making circles in Japan find themselves involved in a sophisticated process of adapting to fast-changing international relations. They have not yet hammered out a coherent concept by which to enhance the role of Japan in world politics.

A066. Kernell, S. (Ed.) **PARALLEL POLITICS: ECONOMIC POLICYMAKING IN JAPAN AND THE UNITED STATES.** Brookings Books, 1990.

A comparison of the Japanese and American political systems affecting policy for business, economics, and trade; one that offers some surprises.

A067. Kesavan, K.V. **JAPAN AND THE TIANANMEN SQUARE INCIDENT: ASPECTS OF THE BILATERAL RELATIONSHIP.** *Asian Survey*, Vol. 30, July 1990, pp. 669–681.

The Tiananmen military crackdown occurred at a time when Tokyo was making efforts to increase its foreign policy options. Japan's response to the turmoil in China may be studied under three broad headings: diplomatic, economic, and political.

A068. Kiener, R. **HOW TOSHIBA TOOK ON WASHINGTON—AND WON.** *Business Tokyo*, Vol. 3, Dec. 1989, pp. 30–33.

Describes the Toshiba sale of sensitive machinery to the Soviet Union. Toshiba's successful handling of the crisis illustrates the crucial role that lobbying plays in Washington's power politics—and confirms Japan's mastery of America's influence-peddling game.

A069. Kim, E. **SOVIET–JAPANESE ECONOMIC INTERACTION AND THE INTERNATIONAL ENVIRONMENT: IMPLICATIONS FOR KOREA–SOVIET ECONOMIC RELATIONS.** Korea and World Affairs, Vol. 13, Fall 1989, pp. 440–461.

Looks at the period since 1972 to examine the influence of superpower relations on Soviet–Japanese economic relations, focusing on Japan's participation in the Siberian Development Projects (SDP).

A070. Kim, H.N. **THE KOREAN MINORITY IN JAPAN.** *Korea and World Affairs*, Vol. 13, Spring 1990, pp.111–136.

The purpose of this paper is to examine the present status of the Korean minority in Japan and to focus on the scope and nature of the problems encountered by the Korean minority in Japan in the post-World War II period.

A071. Kimura, H. **THE SOVIET–JAPANESE TERRITORIAL DISPUTE.** *Harriman Institute Forum*, Vol. 2, June 1989, pp. 1–8.

World War II ended forty-four years ago, yet there still has not been a peace treaty signed between Japan and the Soviet Union. The stumbling block is what the Japanese call the 'Northern Territories' (Hoppo ryodo) problem, or the question of sovereignty of the Norther Territories—the Haboma is a group of islets and the islands of Shikotan, Kunashiri and Etorofu off the northern coast of Hokkaido....Soviet troops occupied the islands, and subsequently the Soviet government incorporate them into the territory of the USSR.

A072. Kohno, M. and Nishizawa, Y. **A STUDY OF THE ELECTORAL BUSINESS CYCLE IN JAPAN: ELECTIONS AND GOVERNMENT SPENDING ON PUBLIC CONSTRUCTION.** *Comparative Politics*, Vol. 22, Jan. 1990, pp. 151–166.

Examines the nature of the electoral business cycle in Japan and seeks to identify the Liberal Democratic Party (LDP) government's attempt to manipulate the economy for electoral purposes. Concludes that one of the LDP's strategies in general elections is to consolidate its own foothold by targeted manipulation of specific economic programs....Hence, the manipulation of public works spending, if carefully targeted at critical electoral districts, becomes an effective measure for the LDP's electoral success.

A073. Koji, H. **A HALF-HEARTED ANTI-APARTHEID POLICY.** *Japan Quarterly*, Vol. 36, July–Sept. 1989, pp. 267–274.

Japan became South Africa's biggest trading partner in 1987 and on Dec. 5, 1988 the United Nations General Assembly debate on comprehensive, compulsory sanctions against the racist Pretoria regime culminated in a resolution that singled out Japan for criticism....There is no denying that Japan has simply failed to come up with any convincing economic sanctions against the Republic of South Africa.

A074. Koppel, B. and Plummer, M. **JAPAN'S ASCENDANCY AS A FOREIGN-AID POWER: ASIAN PERSPECTIVES.** *Asian Survey*, Vol. 29, Nov. 1989, pp. 1043–1056.

The article examines trade, investment, and ODA relationships between Japan and Asia and ask whether from the perspective of developing countries in Asia, do these relationships indicate the emergence of a hegemonic association with Japan? The analysis offered should be taken as suggestive rather than conclusive.

A075. Kuriyama, T. **ASSUMING GLOBAL RESPONSIBILITIES IN TRANSITION PERIOD.** *Economic Eye*, Vol. 11, autumn 1990: pp. 4–8.

In the aftermath of the upheaval in the socialist bloc, the 1990s promise to be a transitional period in the shift to a new global order. Japan's sudden surge in economic power, which has provoked unease and fear in other countries, must be recognized as one of the transition's major causes. Japan must now accept responsibilities commensurate with its new status, shedding its small-country mentality. Together with the United States and Europe, Japan must move quickly to head off the forces of protectionism and economic nationalism.

A076. Lee, C.H. and Yamazawa, I. (Eds.) **THE ECONOMIC DEVELOPMENT OF JAPAN AND KOREA: A PARALLEL WITH LESSONS**. Praeger Publishers, 1990. 205 pp.

Experts from Japan and Korea were invited to write papers on the following six topics and their role in economic development: (l) trade, (2) government, (3) the contribution of imported technology, (4) financial systems and policies, (5) agriculture, and (6) education and society. First, a workshop took place in Seoul and then an international conference was held at the East-West Center in April 1987. Participating in this were scholars from various countries in the Asia-Pacific region whose comments and suggestions contributed greatly to the project. The papers from the conference form the basis of this volume.

A077. Mack, A. and O'Hare, M. **MOSCOW–TOKYO AND THE NORTHERN TERRITORIES DISPUTE.** *Asian Survey*, Vol. 30, Apr. 1990, pp. 380–394.

The most serious barrier today to a major improvement in relations between Tokyo and Moscow is the long-standing and bitter dispute over a number of small islands lying between the northern Japanese island of Hokkaido and the USSR's Kamchatka Peninsula. The territories in question—Etorofu, Kunashiri, Shikotan and the Habomai Islands—are claimed by both the Japanese and the Soviets.

A079. Mansfield, M. **THE U.S. AND JAPAN: SHARING OUR DESTINIES.** *Foreign Affairs*, Vol. 68, Spring 1989, pp. 3–15.

Claims that despite the seemingly endless series of disputes over market access and unfair trade practices, the bilateral relationship between Japan and the U.S. remains strong. Reviews a variety of joint efforts taken in the areas of trade, economic assistance, and cultural exchanges.

A080. Masamichi, I. **CAN THE LDP RECOVER?** *Japan Echo*, Vol. 16, Winter 1990, pp. 9–13.

In the election defeat of July 1989 the LDP lost its majority in the upper house of the National Diet for the first time since it was founded. The purpose of this article is to examine the causes of this stunning defeat and consider whether the party will be able to make a comeback.

A081. Masumi, I. **WHY THE LDP DEBACLE?** *Japan*, Vol. 36, Oct.–Dec. 1989, pp. 386–391.

Examines recent political gains by Japan's Socialist Party. Considers reasons for the trend.

A082. Maull, H.W. **GERMANY AND JAPAN: THE NEW CIVILIAN POWERS.** *Foreign Affairs*, Vol. 69, Winter 1990, pp. 91–106.

The power of Japan and Germany has again become a cause of concern....Some observers fear a return of either state (or both) to traditional temptations of military power politics and suspect that Japan or Germany may revert to challenging the status quo....Others worry about the implications of a changing distribution of economic power....The forces of change in the postwar era, which have worked so powerfully in favor of the West and against the East, are now seen as threatening American control over events.

A083. **MEET WASHINGTON'S NEW MAN IN TOKYO.** *Business Tokyo*, Vol. 3, Oct. 1989, pp. 30,32–33.

Interviews the recently confirmed U.S. Ambassador to Japan. The discussion touches on the issues of trade, the FSX, and the role of Congress in commercial policy toward Japan.

A084. Mendl, W. **STUCK IN A MOULD: THE RELATIONSHIP BETWEEN JAPAN AND THE SOVIET UNION.** *Millennium*, Vol. 18, Winter 1989, pp. 455–478.

The relations between Japan and the Soviet Union remain stuck in a pattern, apparently little affected by the winds of changes. The fact that their shared interests—and there are some—are outweighed by the issues that divide them, may be one explanation of the stalemate in postwar Japanese–Soviet relations....Since 1945 (the relationship) has been influenced by additional factors; the circumstances of the Soviet Union's entry into the war against Japan; the dispute over the Northern Territories....Of these, the territorial issue has become the symbol and the substance of Japan's relationship with its giant northern neighbor.

A085. Michitoshi, T. **THE LIBERAL-DEMOCRATIC PARTY IN CRISIS.** *Japan Quarterly*, Vol. 36, July–Sept. 1989, pp. 244–251.

A086. Miyoshi, M. **TAKING THE LONG VIEW: A FENCE-MENDING PLAN FOR JAPAN–U.S. RELATIONS.** *Speaking of Japan*, Vol. 11, June 1990, pp. 8–11.

Presents the text of a speech by Masaya Muyoshi, President and Director-General, Keidanren, in which he makes recommendations for smoothing the U.S.–Japan trade friction.

A087. Nadell, B. **JAPAN'S POLITICAL STASIS AND THE LIBERAL DEMOCRATIC PARTY.** *Harvard International Review*, Vol. 12, Summer 1990, pp. 38–40.

The ruling party seems to have made no attempt whatsoever to mollify its constituents, other than replacing a few names at the top of the party hierarchy.

A088. Nanto, D.K. **ASIAN RESPONSES TO THE GROWTH OF REGIONAL TRADING BLOCS.** *Looking Ahead and Projection Highlights*, Vol. 11, Jan. 1990, pp. 20–25.

Claims that although Japan and the Asian NIEs (newly industrializing countries) will likely continue to view the growing trading blocs in Europe and North America with concern, they are unlikely to take drastic countermeasures such as forming a bloc on their own. They see existing blocs as somewhat defensive actions against their exports and are confident they can work within those environments, especially if direct foreign investments are not prohibited.

A089. Neff, R., Holden, T. and Buell, B. **CAN JAPAN COPE? WHY THE WORLD HAS SO MUCH RIDING ON ITS RESILIENCY.** *Business Week*, No. 3156, Apr. 23, 1990, 46,48–52,54.

Suddenly, a series of shocks is buffeting the mighty Japanese economy. The stock market plunged 30%. The yen is weakening. Inflation and interest rates are both on the rise. Political leadership is weak. And now some strains are appearing in the nation's normally harmonious social structure. Japan has proved remarkably adaptable to adversity in the past. This time, it may be harder.

A090. Neff, R. and Magnusson, P. **RETHINKING JAPAN: THE NEW, HARDER LINE TOWARD TOKYO.** *Business Week*, No. 3118, Aug. 7, 1989, pp. 44,46–52.

A growing cadre at the highest levels of U.S. government business, and academe is discarding the hope that the Japanese will ever subscribe to free-market rules. If they won't grown more like us, the feelings goes, maybe we can become more like them. Import restrictions and managed trade, the revisionists assert, are games two can play. Includes a Business Week/Harris poll of what 1,250 adult Americans think of Japan Inc.

A091. Nester, W. **JAPAN'S MAINSTREAM PRESS: FREEDOM TO CONFORM?** *Pacific Affairs*, Vol. 62, Spring 1989, pp. 29–39.

Although freedom of the press is constitutionally guaranteed, an analysis of Japan's mainstream press reveals a relatively cohesive news cartel that tends to support the government position on most central issues. Even news of scandals is picked up by the mainstream press only after it has broken elsewhere....The newspapers actually tend to be easily manipulated by the LDP, ministries, or corporate world. This study analyzes the press structure and role in Japan's political system.

A092. Nester, W. **JAPAN'S RECRUIT SCANDAL: GOVERNMENT AND BUSINESS FOR SALE.** *Third World Quarterly*, Vol. 12, Apr. 1990, pp. 91–109.

The Recruit and Uno scandals, and LDP's rapid recovery from them, raise a range of interesting questions about the nature of Japanese politics and power.

A093. Nester, W. **THE THIRD WORLD IN JAPANESE FOREIGN POLICY.** *Millennium*, Journal of International Studies, Vol. 18, No. 3, 1989, pp. 377–398.

Japan's foreign policy toward the Third World is explored in three parts. The first part puts Tokyo's Third World policy in the context of its overall foreign policy. The second part analyzes Japan's economic interests in trade, investments and aid in different regions of the Third World. The third section looks at how skillful Japanese diplomacy in several regional or bilateral conflicts effectively secured Japan's economic and political interests in those respective areas.

A094. Nester, W. and Ampiah, K. **JAPAN'S OIL DIPLOMACY: TATEMAE AND HONNE.** *Third World Quarterly*, Vol. 11, Jan. 1989, pp. 72–88.

Attempts to distinguish between the "honne" (reality) and the "tatemae" (principle) of Japanese policy toward the Middle East. Discusses Japanese diplomacy in dealing with the oil embargo of 1973, the Iranian hostage crisis, and the Iran–Iraq war, concluding that Japan has consistently followed its economic interests.

A095. **NEW MEN, OLD DEBTS, NEW MASKS.** *Business Tokyo,* Vol. 3, Jan. 1989, pp. 6–11.

In a series of short articles Business Tokyo summarizes the results of interviews and surveys that canvassed the opinions of opinion leaders in Japan and also selected American businessmen, politicians, and economists. Asks will the new president be able to break away from old policies and find new solutions to the problems facing the two nations? Or is the change in the White House—as many on both sides of the Pacific fear—just a new mask for the same kind of thinking that led America into these difficulties in the first place?

A096. Okawara, Y. **TO AVOID ISOLATION: AN AMBASSADOR'S VIEW OF U.S./JAPANESE RELATIONS.** University of South Carolina Press, 1990, 182 pp.

Mike Mansfield, former U.S. Ambassador to Japan, describes relations between the United States and Japan as "the most important bilateral relationship in the world, bar none." *To Avoid Isolation* affords readers the opportunity to look at this important relationship as viewed through the eyes of the Japanese Ambassador to the United States during the Carter and Reagan administrations. In this book, Okawara examines the problems developing across the Pacific Ocean and the causes for various frictions, particularly in the economic field.

A097. Okita, S. **JAPAN IN THE WORLD ECONOMY OF THE 1980s.** Univ. of Tokyo Press (Columbia Univ. Press), 1989, ISBN 0-86008-451-5, 270 pp.

A098. Okita, S. **JAPAN'S ROLE IN ASIA–PACIFIC COOPERATION.** *Annals of the American Academy of Political and Social Science,* Vol. 513, Jan. 1991, pp. 25–37.

Claims that Japan needs to respond to trade imbalances and protectionist sentiments in the U.S. Calls for Japan to strengthen the international trading arrangements by promoting Asia–Pacific cooperation premised on openness. Given the region's great internal diversity, Asia–Pacific economic cooperation can well serve as a model for international economic coordination.

A099. Okonogi, M. **THE POLITICAL DYNAMICS OF JAPAN–NORTH KOREA RELATIONS.** *Korea and World Affairs,* Vol. 13, Summer 1989, pp. 331–346.

What the Japanese government, while being careful not to touch the wrong nerve in South Korea, is seeking to establish is not a bilateral but trilateral coexistence among Tokyo, Seoul and Pyongyang.

A100. Orr, R.M., Jr. **COLLABORATION OR CONFLICT? FOREIGN AID AND U.S.–JAPAN RELATIONS.** *Pacific Affairs,* Vol. 62, Winter 1989–90, pp. 476–489.

The article focuses on three questions: first, how different is Japan's approach to foreign assistance from that of the United States? Secondly, how has this created bilateral conflict? And third, has there been cooperation in the area and if so, what kind?

A101. Orr, R.M. **JAPAN: ITS CHANGING FOREIGN AID POLICY.** Columbia Univ. Pr., 1990, ISBN 0-231-07046-2, 192 pp.

Focusing on the role that foreign aid played on the economic and political relations between the United States and Japan, Professor Orr details the Japanese aid program—the lengthy decision-making process that the Japanese government requires—analyzing its influence on the United States and the United States' influence on it.

A102. Orr, R.M., Jr. **THE RISING SUM: WHAT MAKES JAPAN GIVE?** *International Economy*, Vol. 3, Sept.–Oct. 1989, pp. 80–83.

Describes the scope and type of Japanese financial aid to developing countries and the motivations underlying Japan's recent expansion of its foreign aid programs. Argues that Tokyo's aid efforts are essentially directed at addressing Japan's own 'vulnerabilities,' rather than those in developing countries, makes it possible to understand how aid policy could change from an export promotion device to a mechanism aimed at protecting vital resources to a system of responding to foreign expectations of Japan.

A103. Pierce, J.C., Lovrich, N.P. and Matsuoka, M. **SUPPORT FOR CITIZEN PARTICIPATION: A COMPARISON OF AMERICAN AND JAPANESE CITIZENS, ACTIVISTS AND ELITES.** *Western Political Quarterly*, Vol. 43, Mar. 1990, pp. 39–59.

This paper examines the dynamics underlying contemporary demands for broader citizen involvement in environmental policy formation processes in two postindustrial nations. The subjects of study are Japanese and American citizens, activists, and elected/administrative elites in two comparable locations of recent high public activism concerning environmental issues.

A104. **POWER AND ITS PERILS.** *Business Tokyo*, Vol. 3, May 1989, pp. 5–9.

Examines the status of events in Japanese politics in the post-Recruit period. Considers implications for U.S.–Japanese relations.

A105. Quinn, S. **BLEAK PROSPECTS: ISLAND DISPUTE CONTINUES TO MAR SOVIET–JAPANESE TIES.** *Far Eastern Economic Review*, Vol. 144, July 20, 1989, pp. 30–32.

Japan claims these islands—Iturup (Etorofu), Kunashir, Shikotan and the Habomai group—as its 'northern territories'....The Japanese have refused to sign a peace treaty formally ending World War II with the Soviet Union until the islands are returned.

A106. Rix, A. **JAPAN'S FOREIGN AID POLICY: A CAPACITY FOR LEADERSHIP?** *Pacific Affairs*, Vol. 62, Winter 1989–90, pp. 461–475.

In 1989 Japan was set to become the largest donor of foreign aid within the QECD's....Development Assistance Committee (DAC)....This paper is concerned with Japan's actions as a donor, and whether Japan has been able to show 'leadership' in aid policy. Has Japan taken positive initiatives in aid? Has Japan helped shape international aid policy?

A107. Rosecrance, R. and Taw. J. **JAPAN AND THE THEORY OF INTERNATIONAL LEADERSHIP.** *World Politics,* Vol. 42, Jan. 1990, pp. 184–209.

Japan is doing now, against its will, many of the same things that have led to hegemonic decline in the past. In fact, the country's relative growth in power, while still increasing, is already doing so at a decreasing rate. There are good reasons for Japan's present behavior: the leading economic power cannot escape the dangers of a possible collapse in the world trading and financial system....Japan must bail out the system even though the result is slower growth and excessive consumption. In this way, Tokyo is beginning to help the world, but perhaps unwittingly contributing to Japan's own ultimate decline.

A108. Rosett, C. **JAPAN'S RECRUIT SCANDAL IN CONTEXT.** *Wall Street Journal,* Apr. 10, 1989, A14.

Consider the implications of the Recruit Company scandal in Japan's politics.

A109. Russell, D. **AMERICA'S HOLLOW VICTORY.** *Business Tokyo,* Vol. 4, June, 1990, pp. 32–35.

Examines the results of the April 1990 SII talks. Debunks the view that the talks were a success for the U.S. Argues that, in fact, Japan's major SII concessions....were either relatively minor or more beneficial to Japan than to America. More substantial were Japan's concessions on Congress's three 'Super 301' targets (supercomputers, satellites and wood products), with Japan agreeing to shop more at the international supermarket instead of patronizing only domestic vendors. Even so, the agreements fell short of the U.S. ideal.

A110. Ryang, S.S. **ETHNO-POLITICAL COMMUNITY OF 'NORTH' KOREANS IN JAPAN.** *International Migration,* Vol. 28, Mar. 1990, pp. 105–112.

Examines both the degree of assimilation of Japan's North Korean minority and the degree of their nationalistic identification with both North and South Korea.

A111. Samuels, R.J. and Whipple, B.C. **THE FSX AND JAPAN'S STRATEGY FOR AEROSPACE.** *Technology Review,* Vol. 92, Oct. 1989, pp. 43–51.

After a 40-year preoccupation with commercial economic development, Japan is now expanding defense production to compete effectively in aerospace.

A112. Sato, S. **THE U.S.–JAPAN ALLIANCE UNDER CHANGING INTERNATIONAL RELATIONS.** *Washington Quarterly,* Vol. 13, Summer 1990, pp. 69–83.

In order to maintain and further develop the U.S.–Japanese alliance, it is of special importance that both nations share the same perceptions vis-a-vis major international trends, the recognition that they have large common interest, and the determination to divide between them, commensurate to their respective positions and abilities, the responsibilities and burdens of achieving goals of mutual interest.

A113. Sato, T., Momose, T. and Williams, D. **THE GORBACHEV REVOLUTION AND JAPAN.** *Tokyo Business Today,* Vol. 58, Mar. 1990, pp. 26–31.

Examines Japanese economic relations with the Soviet Union and Eastern Europe. Provides a brief overview of Japan's trade with and investment in the Soviet bloc countries. Describes the mounting skepticism among Japanese business interests over the market potential of Eastern Europe and the Soviet Union.

A114. Sayle, M. **GOVERNMENT BY SCANDAL.** *Business Tokyo,* Vol. 3, May 1989, pp. 18–21.

Over the years, Japanese prosecutors have uncovered many instances of political corruption. The Recruit affair, though, could be a major turning point in the way money and influence are bartered among businessmen, bureaucrats and politicians.

A115. Sayle, M. **TROUBLE ON THE ORIENTAL EXPRESS. THE CRISES IN CHINA AND JAPAN.** *National Interest,* No. 18, Winter 1989–90, pp. 29–45.

China and Japan set out on a long search for modernization without sacrificing their national essence of identity, a search still far from complete in either country. Both recognized the capitalist trading system as both the likeliest mechanism of modernization and the greatest of all threats to their societies. Both sought to use Western ideas, suitably modified, to defend themselves against the overwhelming Western threat.

A116. Schlosstein, S.B. **THE NEW McCARTHYISM.** *International Economy,* Vol. 4, Apr.–May 1990, pp. 32–36.

Describes the views and mutual disdain of the revisionist and apologist views of U.S.–Japan relations. Argues that this feud has poised the process of building a common ground between them and prevented the debate from moving forward. Suggests a round table discussion to air their policy differences on four key themes: trade and foreign investment; market dynamics; counter-competitive strategies; and measures to strengthen the U.S. position.

A117. Segal, G. **NORTHEAST ASIA: ALL ABOARD THE DETENTE TRAIN?** *World Today,* Vol. 46, Mar. 1990, pp. 49–53.

The Soviet Union and China warmed up for their normalization of relations in 1989....North Korea has made some noises but there has been no significant progress so far (and) Soviet–Japanese relations, has lagged behind the pace of the improved political climate elsewhere in Northeast Asia.

A118. Shintaro, I. **LEARNING TO SAY NO TO AMERICA.** *Japan Echo,* Vol. 17, Spring 1990, pp. 29–35.

The greatest problem is not the strength of the Japanese economy but the weakness of the U.S. competitive position. American attempts to treat the problem only through changes on the Japanese side will thus not have the intended results....The time has come for the people in both countries to....put together a new framework of bilateral cooperation.

A119. Simon, S.W. **THE SINO-SOVIET FUTURE: SOME PRC PERSPECTIVES.** *Third World Quarterly,* Vol. 11, July 1989, pp. 85–106.

This article attempts to project the PRC's policies towards the USSR into the early 1990s and to assess the effects of Sino-Soviet relations on other major targets of PRC foreign policy, including the U.S.A. Japan, and such important neighbors as Indochina and the Koreans.

A120. Smith, C. and Hanson, R. **LIFE AFTER HARAKIRI.** *Far Eastern Economic Review*, Vol. 145, Aug. 10, 1989, pp. 15–18.
Examines the status of Japan's political parties and considers political changes in that country.

A121. Solovyov, N. **ON THE JAPANESE ISLANDS.** *International Affairs (Moscow)*, Sept. 1989, pp. 111–116.
The Soviet Ambassador to Japan is interviewed by International Affairs.

A122. Stockwin, J.A.A., Rix, A., George, A., Horne, J., Itō, D. and Collick, M. **DYNAMIC AND IMMOBILIST POLITICS IN JAPAN.** Honolulu: University of Hawaii Press, 1988, 342 pp.
Chapters on parties, bureaucracy, interest groups, the economy and the financial system combine with case studies on policy-making in the fields of administrative reform, social welfare, defence and trade. The book casts doubt on 'consensus' view about Japan and shows that within a strong and stable political system there are many conflicting—and often immobilizing—pressures to work.

A123. Stokes, B. **WHO'S STANDING TALL?** *National Journal*, Vol. 21, Oct. 21, 1989, pp. 2568–2573.
American revisionists want the U.S. government to get tough with Japan, but it's the Japanese who have the economic muscle now, and they no longer will bow to Washington's dictates.

A124. **SYMPOSIUM: THE SHO SATO MEMORIAL CONFERENCE: JAPAN, THE UNITED STATES AND PACIFIC OCEAN RESOURCES.** *Ecology Law Quarterly*, Vol. 16, No. 1, 1989, whole issue, p. 359.
Partial contents—Japan, the United States, and the Pacific since 1945: and overview, by A. Watanabe. In the realm of diplomacy and fish: some reflections on the International Convention on High Seas Fisheries in the North Pacific Ocean and the Law of the Sea negotiation, by W.C. Herrington. Antarctic resources and international law: Japan, and the United States, and the future of Antarctica, by R. Friedheim and T. Akaha. Japan and the Antarctic Treaty system, by C.C. Joyner. The United States and Japan in relation to the resources, the environment, and the people of the Pacific Island region, by J.M. Van Dyke. The U.S.–Korean fishing rights dispute in the North Pacific Ocean, by C.-H. Park. Japanese environmental law and ocean resources, by N. Kumamoto. International sanctions, ocean management, and the law of the sea: a study of denial of access to fisheries, by D.D. Caron. Pacific Ocean resources: the new regionalism and the global system, by S. Riesenfeld.

A125. **SYMPOSIUM—WHALES AND WHALING: CURRENT PROBLEMS AND FUTURE PROSPECTS.** *Denver Journal of International Law and Policy*, Vol. 17, Winter 1989, pp. 247–393.

Contents—Introduction: preserving whales in a world of sovereign states, by R. Falk. Whales: towards a developing right of survival as part of an ecosystem, by S.K. Chopra. The use of domestic measures to enforce international whaling agreements: critical perspective, by D.M. Wilkinson. Enforcing the international convention for the regulation of whaling: the Pelly and Packwood–Magnuson Amendments, by G.S. Martin, Jr. and J.W. Brennan. The "whale war" between Japan and the United States: problems and prospects, by K. Sumi. Aboriginal subsistence whaling: the right of Inuit to hung whales and implications for international environmental law, by N.C. Doubleday. International regulation of whaling (book review), by S.K. Chopra.

A126. Takenaka, H. **JAPAN'S ROLE AND RESPONSIBILITIES IN THE WORLD ECONOMIC SYSTEM.** *Washington Quarterly*, Vol. 13, Summer 1990, pp. 107–120.

Former Japanese Ministry of Finance official considers the role Japan should play in the world economic system. Also examines bilateral U.S.–Japanese economic frictions and options to manage these problems more effectively.

A127. Takeshi, S. **THE LDP TEETERS IN THE POLITICAL BALANCE.** *Japan Quarterly*, Vol. 36, Oct.–Dec. 1989, pp. 375–380.

Examines recent trends in Japanese politics and discusses popular support for the Liberal Democratic Party (LDP).

A128. Tamamoto, M. **JAPAN'S SEARCH FOR A WORLD ROLE.** *World Policy Journal*, Vol. 7, Summer 1990, pp. 483–520.

Japan, it is assumed, will at some point move more aggressively to translate the enormous economic wealth it has amassed over the past decade into political and military power....Its new assertiveness and greater independence internationally, it is feared, will harm U.S. interests and undermine global stability.

A129. Tarnoff, P. **AMERICA'S NEW SPECIAL RELATIONSHIPS.** *Foreign Affairs*, Vol. 69, Summer 1990, pp. 67–80.

Asserts that Washington should move quickly to fully engage Tokyo and Bonn (or rather Berlin, when it becomes capital of a united Germany) in all major discussions about the shape of the post-Cold War world. While the United States, Germany and Japan must avoid fueling the suspicions of other governments that they intend to constitute a new tripartite 'directorate,' it is strongly in the American interest to assure that a shared vision informs policies in Washington, Tokyo and Berlin.

A130. Taro, Y. **THE RECRUIT SCANDAL: LEARNING FROM THE CAUSES OF CORRUPTION.** *Journal of Japanese Studies*, Vol. 16, Winter 1990, pp. 93–114.

Describes the stock gift scandal that shook the Japanese government in 1989. Charges that the underlying cause is that politics costs money. As long as it remains impossible to get elected unless you collect the necessary money, the most eloquent preaching about ethics is only going to Fall on deaf ears. And if we just leave things as they are, capable people with any ethical sense will disappear from the political stage entirely.

A131. Terumasa, N. **SAYING YES TO THE JAPAN–U.S. PARTNERSHIP.** *Japan Echo*, Vol. 17, Spring 1990, pp. 36–42.

A critique of 'No' to ieru Nihon (A Japan that Can Say No; Tokyo: Kobunsha, 1989), coauthored by Sony Chairman Morita Akio and the political Ishihara Shintaro....Examines Ishihara's position as expressed in the book and in recent magazine articles....Offering his own thoughts on his perception of the course Japan should take in international society.

A132. Tharp, M. **JAPAN'S BACKYARD STRATEGY.** *International Economy*, Vol. 4, Feb.–Mar. 1990, pp. 62–65.

With U.S.–Japan relations at a post-war ebb, it is tempting to seek historical precedent. Half a century ago, of course, Japan was well underway with its Greater East Asia Co-Prosperity Sphere, an oriental Lebensraum spread much more by sword than by economic fiat. Today, Japan's influence in Asia is close to surpassing that of the U.S. and already exceeds that of the Soviet Union.

A133. Trezise, P.H. **JAPAN, THE ENEMY?** *Brookings Review*, Vol. 8, Winter 1989–90, pp. 3–13.

The United States does have problems in its economic relations with Japan. Not all of them are trivial. But do they make Japan a....danger to American interests or security? Or have we in fact magnified these problems out of all proportion?

A134. Uchida, T. **JAPAN AND THE ARAB WORLD: AN ECONOMIC PERSPECTIVE.** *American–Arab Affairs*, No. 32, Spring 1990, pp. 27–42.

Spokesman for Japan's Ministry of Foreign Affairs describes trade and investment relations between Japan and the Middle East, including levels of official development assistance. Includes accompanying articles by Ryozo Kato (Japan's political role in the Middle East, past and present) and by Michael Collins and Julia Ackerman (The United States, Japan, and the Gulf: common interests, potential competition).

A135. **U.S.A. LOOKS AT THE WORLD (AND) THE WORLD LOOKS AT THE U.S.A.** *USA Today* (magazine), Vol. 119, July 1990, pp. 38–41.

Contents—American–Japanese–European relations: a view from Washington, by C.J. Brown. U.S.–Japanese economic relations: a view from Tokyo, by N. Akao.

A136. **U.S. CONGRESS. HOUSE. COMMITTEE ON FOREIGN AFFAIRS.**

Congress and Foreign Policy 1989, Washington, G.P.O., 1990, p. 139. Contents—The role of Congress in foreign policy in 1989. Congress and the transformation of Eastern Europe in 1989. Japanese FSX fighter controversy. Congress and policy toward Central America in 1989. Foreign assistance: congressional initiatives to reform U.S. foreign aid in 1989. Congress and international environmental issues in 1989.

A137. **U.S. CONGRESS. HOUSE. COMMITTEE ON INTERIOR AND INSULAR AFFAIRS. SUBCOMMITTEE ON INSULAR AND INTERNATIONAL AFFAIRS.**

To amend the Organic Act of Guam. Hearing, 101st Congress, 1st session on H.R. 2024, July 27, 1989, Washington, G.P.O., 1990, p. 257. Serial no. 101–20.

A138. **U.S. CONGRESS. HOUSE. JOINT ECONOMIC COMMITTEE.**
Japan's economic challenge; study papers submitted to the Joint Economic Committee, Congress of the United States. Washington, G.P.O., 1990, p. 498. (Print, Senate, 101st Congress, 2nd session, joint committee print 5. Prt. 101–121). The current study examines Japan's emergence as an economic superpower. In order to understand this nation's impressive performance and growing global role, there are assessments of its policies, structure, and domestic and international trends. Partial contents—Framework of economic policy. Government and business. Balance and investment. Human resources. Science and technology. National security and foreign aid. International economic relations.

A139. **U.S. CONGRESS. SENATE. COMMITTEE ON FOREIGN RELATIONS.**
Major issues of U.S. policy in East Asia; a staff report. Washington, G.P.O., 1989, p. 10 (Print, Senate, 101st Congress, 1st session, committee print S. Prt. 101–21). A visit to four nations in East Asia in late 1988 for the purpose of assessing the impact of major developments on U.S. policy in the region.

A140. **U.S. GENERAL ACCOUNTING OFFICE.**
Economic assistance: integration of Japanese aid and trade policies; report to the Chairman, Subcommittee on Economic Resources and Competitiveness, Joint Economic Committee, U.S. Congress, May 24, 1990, Washington, G.A.O., 1990, p. 21. Examines the extent to which Japan integrates its foreign economic and policy with its foreign trade policy.

A141. **U.S.–JAPAN RELATIONS.** *Gist*, June 1989: 1–2.
Details U.S.–Japanese economic, military and foreign relations.

A142. Valencia, M.J. **NORTHEAST ASIA: PETROLEUM POTENTIAL, JURISDICTIONAL CLAIMS, AND INTERNATIONAL RELATIONS.** *Ocean Development and International Law*, Vol. 20, No. 1, 1989, pp. 35–61.
In East Asian seas, many overlapping claims or areas of unresolved boundaries encompass basins with good petroleum potential. They include the Tsushima Basin (Japan/South Korea), the Korea Bay (China/North Korea), and those in the Yellow (China/South Korea) and East China seas (China/Japan). In Northwest Asia, where state relations are deeply divided, such maritime issues or their resolution could take on much wider political import. The political context of the disputes is described and various solutions including joint development are elaborated for the disputes between China and Japan, and China and South Korea.

A143. Vernon, R. **THE JAPAN–U.S. BILATERAL RELATIONSHIP: ITS ROLE IN THE GLOBAL ECONOMY.** *Washington Quarterly*, Vol. 13, Summer 1990, pp. 57–68.
Comments on the likely role of Japan in the global political and economic scene in the near future. Claims that bilateral relations between Japan and the U.S. promise to remain critical for both countries. Dispute settlement and policy issues between the two giants would be better handled by existing multilateral institutions than through bilateral channels.

A144. Vlastos, S. **PEASANT PROTESTS AND UPRISINGS IN TOKUGAWA JAPAN.** Univ. of California Pr., 1990, ISBN 0-520-07203-0, 184 pp.

A145. Wanner, B. **DOMESTIC AND INTERNATIONAL FACTORS CHALLENGE KAIFU ADMINISTRATION.** Washington, Japan Economic Institute, 1990, p. 15 (JEI report no. 42A).

Notes that while some analysts now believe that Mr. Kaifu could serve a full, two-year term, this assessment may change in the coming months....Mr. Kaifu had planned this Fall to tackle some difficult domestic issues, including the electoral system, the consumption tax and land prices. However, an even tougher leadership test will come in pushing through legislation that would allow a broader Japanese response to global crises.

A146. Watanabe, P. and Imperial, L.E. **THE PAST AS PRESENT: UNITED STATES–JAPAN RELATIONS AND THE POLITICS OF THE TOSHIBA SCANDAL.** *Business in the Contemporary World*, Vol. 2, Summer 1990, pp. 84–94.

This article, by closely examining the Toshiba case, explores some of the factors that shape American attitudes toward Japan and the policies that accompany these feelings.

A147. Watson, R. **THE COP AND THE BENEFACTOR.** *Newsweek*, Vol. 113, Feb. 6, 1989, pp. 36,40.

Discusses the rise of Japan's nonmilitary foreign aid to a level exceeding the level of the U.S. Examines concerns that in aid as in trade, Japan will continue to advance, sometimes to America's disadvantage. And as long as military security is a top concern, Washington will probably be left holding that bag—playing policeman while Japan plays benefactor.

A148. Weatherford, M.S. and Fukui, H. **DOMESTIC ADJUSTMENT TO INTERNATIONAL SHOCKS IN JAPAN AND THE UNITED STATES.** *International Organization*, Vol. 43, autumn 1989, pp. 585–623.

Explains how the U.S. and Japan responded to the energy supply shocks of 1973 and 1979. How promptly and accurately did the governments diagnose and respond to the stagflationary effects of the shocks? How coherent and consistent were their macroeconomic policies?

A149. Yakushiji, T. **POLITICAL FACTORS IN SHAPING JAPAN'S FOREIGN ECONOMIC POLICY.** *International Spectator*, Vol. 24, July–Dec. 1989, pp. 208–213.

Concludes that Japan's postwar grafted democracy, reflecting early postwar international politics, gave birth to a new type of local interest oriented politician....Simultaneously, the exbureaucrat politicians who were once in the mainstream of the LDP faded out as bureaucrats successfully implemented postwar recovery....The result is that no organization or subnational sector is left with sufficient power and prestige to take responsibility for directing the nation's external economic policies.

A150. Yasutomo, D.T. **WHY AID? JAPAN AS AN AID GREAT POWER.** Public Affairs, Vol. 62, Winter 1989–90, pp. 490–503.

The rapid rise of Japan's economic assistance policy in the 1980s is one of the most striking and surprising developments in Japanese foreign policy....Within the previous decade Japan had become the second largest aid-giving nation, second only to the United States, and enters the 1990s in the number one position.

A151. Zagoria, D.S. **SOVIET POLICY IN EAST ASIA: A NEW BEGINNING?** *Foreign Affairs*, Vol. 68, No. 1, 1989, pp. 120–138.

Under Mikhail Gorbachev the Soviet Union has greatly increased its efforts to improve relations with the countries of East Asia....(and) may well succeed in normalizing relations with East Asia during the next few years. Moscow now seeks to increase, not to reduce, Soviet influence abroad. Thus, this new Soviet moderation may actually result in a less aggressive strategy but more active and effective Soviet diplomacy. Considers Soviet relations with China, Japan, and South Korea.

A152. Zhao, J.Q. **INFORMAL PLURALISM AND JAPANESE POLITICS: SINO-JAPANESE RAPPROCHEMENT REVISITED.** *Journal of Northeast Asian Studies*, Vol. 8, Summer 1989, pp. 65–83.

This study attempts to take the 1972 Sino-Japanese rapprochement as a case study on the pluralistic nature of Japanese politics.

A153. Zhao, J.Q. **POLITICS OF JAPAN–CHINA TRADE NEGOTIATIONS.** *Asian Profile*, Vol. 18, Apr. 1990, pp. 97–115.

Examines the four major economic agreements between Japan and China (trade, aviation, maritime transportation, and fisheries) concluded after the 1972 normalization. Focuses on the role played by the bureaucracy and the ruling Liberal Democratic Party (LDP), and the interaction between the two.

A154. Zinsmeister, K. **SHADOWS ON THE RISING SUN.** *American Enterprise*, Vol. 1, May–June 1990, pp. 52–61.

Japan's present-day triumphs mask problems with long-term political, economic, and cultural implications.

B. TRADE POLICY

B001. Akira, K. **THE ASIAN NIEs AS TRADING PARTNERS.** *Japan Quarterly,* Vol. 36, July–Sept. 1989, pp. 263–266.

Discusses the recent rapid rise in Japanese imports of manufactured goods from the newly industrialized economics (NIEs) of Asia. Also discusses the NIEs dependence on the U.S. market. Concludes that if the Asian NIEs are able to learn from Japan's past experience by increasing their international competitiveness and bolstering domestic demand, they will have plenty of maneuverability in responding to U.S. requests to appreciate their currencies and open their markets.

B002. Averyt, W.F. **MANAGING PUBLIC POLICY ABROAD: FOREIGN CORPORATE REPRESENTATION IN WASHINGTON.** *Columbia Journal of World Business,* Vol. 25, Fall 1990, pp. 32–41.

Predicts that corporate representation in Washington by foreign companies will continue to grow. Claims that America's two largest partners, Canada and Japan, provide an interesting contrast, with Japan showing greater representation although Canada remains the larger trade partner of the U.S. Japanese realization of the differences in the US policy environment and emphasis on the importance of strategic information may help to explain the difference.

B003. Cohen, S.D. **UNITED STATES–JAPAN TRADE RELATIONS.** In International Trade: the Changing Role of the United States. New York: Academy of Political Science, 1990, pp. 122–136.

Examines some of the problems behind America's trade relations with Japan, concluding that American industry will not become more competitive in the near future. Regrettably, in its successful but short-sighted pursuits of profit and consumption maximization, America cannot be bothered to respond More effectively to the long-term challenges of the alternative model of capitalist power being pursued in Japan. Also regrettably, Japan is not likely to find increased economic success a reason to become truly less insular.

B004. **COUNCIL REVIEWS TRADE POLICIES OF CANADA, HONG KONG, JAPAN AND NEW ZEALAND** GATT Focus, No. 74, Sept. 1990, pp. 2–10,12.

Examines the trade policies of four members of the General Agreement on Tariffs and Trade (GATT). Comments on such factors as tariff levels, import licensing, agricultural subsidies, and government marketing boards.

B005. Dornbusch, R. **THE SII TALKS ARE A JOKE** *International Economy,* Vol. 4, Feb.–Mar 1990, pp. 47–49.

Argues that the Structural Impediments Initiative (SII) is yet another misdirected attempt to come to grips with the large U.S. trade deficit and the barriers to the Japanese markets. Like previous initiatives, it creates expectations that cannot possibly be fulfilled, inappropriate mechanisms to remedy U.S. trade problems and unproductive friction.

B006. Elving, R.D. **TRADE MOOD TURNS HAWKISH AS FRUSTRATION BUILDS.** *Congressional Quarterly Weekly Report*, Vol. 48, Mar 31, 1990, pp. 965–971.

Claims that congressional frustration with the trade deficit will probably not be translated into tough new action. The congressional calendar is nearly full for the year and the 1988 trade act is just moving into its enforcement phase. Includes a calendar of the major trade deadlines through the Summer of 1990.

B007. Encarnation, D.J. and Mason, M. **NEITHER MITI NOR AMERICA: THE POLITICAL ECONOMY OF CAPITAL LIBERALIZATION IN JAPAN.** *International Organization*, Vol. 44, Winter 1990, pp. 25–54.

Claims that no industrialized country has so adamantly denied multinational corporations (MNCs) access to domestic markets as Japan, where industrial oligopolists and regulatory agencies have prevented rival MNCs from profiting from the nation's prosperity. Claims that neither MITI's administrative guidance nor America's official pressure could alter the pace of foreign direct investment.

B008. Fallows, J. **GETTING ALONG WITH JAPAN.** *Atlantic Monthly*, Vol. 264, Dec. 1989, pp. 53–56,60,62–64.

Claims it's time for America to stop trying to solve its economic problems by demanding that the Japanese change their ways. Without blaming or hectoring any other country, America must put its own house in order. Examines a variety of policies that could be adopted by the U.S., including managed trade and across-the-board tariffs on Japanese products.

B009. Fallows, J. **STANDING UP TO JAPAN.** *Los Angeles Times Magazine*, Vol. 5, Mar. 12, 1989, pp. 10–14.

Argues that the United States cannot reverse its decline relative to Japan by becoming more like the Japanese. Concludes that flexibility is the ultimate U.S. weapon against the Asian economies whereas the Asians discipline, order, and obedience would spell stagnation for America.

B010. **FORUM: JAPAN–U.S. RELATIONS.** *Congressional Research Service Review*, Vol. 10, July 1989, pp. 1–23.

Contents—A more open Japanese market?, by R.A. Ahearn. Japan–U.S. trade: looking ahead, by W.H. Cooper. Technology policy in Japan and the Unites States, by G.J. McLoughlin. Japanese investment in the United States, by J.K. Jackson. Japan's emergence as a leading foreign aid donor, by L.K. Nowels. Japan's expanding economic role and influence in Asia, by R.P. Cronin. Burden sharing and power sharing, by L.A. Niksch. Japan and an East Asian trading bloc, by D.K. Nanto.

B011. Friman, H.R. **PATCHWORK PROTECTIONISM:TEXTILE TRADE POLICY IN THE UNITED STATES, JAPAN, AND WEST GERMANY.** Cornell Univ. Pr., 1990, ISBN 0-8014-2423-2, 209 pp.

B012. Hale, D.D. **GLOBAL FINANCE AND THE RETREAT TO MANAGED TRADE.** *Harvard Business Review*, Vol. 68, Jan.–Feb. 1990, pp. 150–162.

Asserts that the rise of Japanese financial power and the contradictions of U.S. economic policy are weakening the competitive position of the U.S. financial services industry—one of the few sectors where the United States still regards itself as more creative, more sophisticated, and more aggressive than its foreign rivals. As a consequence, the United States may soon face the same market erosion in financial services that has afflicted its producers of machine tools, automobiles, and semiconductors.

B013. Hickok, S. **JAPANESE TRADE BALANCE ADJUSTMENT TO YEN APPLICATION.** *Federal Reserve Bank of New York Quarterly Review*, Vol. 14, autumn 1989, pp. 33–47.

The primary focus of this article is Japan's real trade balance. The article begins with an accounting of the starting base, demand growth, and relative price factors that helped shape Japan's real trade balance evolution. Subsequent sections treat the influence of both Japan's distinctive commodity composition and domestic and foreign demand growth on Japan's trade performance. Also examined in some detail is the charge in Japan's relative price position, broken down into its components—nominal appreciation, unit labor cost, profit margins, and raw material input prices.

B014. Humphreys, D. **TOWARDS AN EEC MINERALS POLICY?** *Resources Policy*, Vol. 19, Mar. 1990, pp. 35–46.

Despite being the world's largest consumer of non-fuel minerals the EEC does not have a common minerals policy. The EEC's position is assessed and compared with those of the U.S.A. and Japan. Moves towards the establishment of a minerals policy, which have been reinforced by changes in the composition of the EEC and by the approach of the single market in 1933, are traced from the mid-1970s, concluding with a description of a major new initiative launched in 1989.

B015. Kingery, J.C. **THE U.S.–JAPAN SEMICONDUCTOR ARRANGEMENT AND THE GATT: OPERATING IN A LEGAL VACUUM.** *Stanford Journal of International Law*, Vol. 25, Spring 1989, pp. 467–497.

Article looks at the U.S.–Japan Semiconductor Arrangement and at objections raised by other nations that such an agreement is inconsistent with GATT rules and may actually create a cartel.

B016. Komiya, R. and Wakasugi, R. **JAPAN'S FOREIGN DIRECT INVESTMENT.** *Annals of the American Academy of Political and Social Science*, Vol. 513, Jan. 1991, pp. 48–61.

Offers a brief historical overview of Japanese foreign investment. Claims that Japanese subsidiaries are not yet bringing substantial profits to their parents but that in the next few years they will become more profitable and will be run more and more as part of the global strategies of their parents.

B017. Korte, K.-R. **JAPAN AND THE SINGLE EUROPEAN MARKET.** *Aussenpolitik*, Vol. 40, No. 4, 1989, pp. 397–407.

Looks at the likelihood of a Fortress Europe developing out of the 1992 integrated market plan and the likely Japanese response. Predicts that Japanese investments will expand as an alternative to direct exports. Japan fears that the various trade barriers of the individual member countries will simply be brought into harmony with one another.

B018. Kostecki, M.M. **ELECTRONICS TRADE POLICIES IN THE 1980s.** *Journal of World Trade*, Vol. 23, Feb. 1989, pp. 17–35.

The electronics industry plays a strategic role in countries' efforts to maintain and increase their competitiveness and in shaping the new 'information society.' Over the last decade or so the electronics sector has been the scene of particularly active, and frequently controversial, trade policies. This overview identifies the main features of those policies and points out a number of problems that electronics trade policies create for the multilateral trading system.

B019. Lincoln, E. **U.S.-JAPANESE TRADE TALKS: HOPE FOR PROGRESS.** Washington: Heritage Foundation, 1990, 9 pp.

Claims that tariffs have come down, the quotas have been eliminated, and yet, if one looks at the trade data, one sees that Japan behaves very differently from most other countries. The author's interest lies particularly in two statistics—one is the ratio of manufactured imports to gross national product (GNP), and the other is an indicator of what economists call intra-industry trade.

B020. Lincoln, E.J. **JAPAN'S UNEQUAL TRADE.** Washington: Brookings Institution, 1990, 223 pp.

Examines Japan's unusual patterns of trade: a low level of manufactured imports and a relative absence of intra-industry trade. The author looks at the question of access to Japanese markets, Japan's pattern of trade on imports, and the consequences of large trade and current-account imbalances. He argues against the United States abandoning its free-trade ideal and offers suggestions for applying pressure to encourage greater real access to Japanese markets.

B021. Martin, J. **TRIVIALIZING THE U.S.–JAPAN DIALOGUE.** *International Economy*, Vol. 4, Apr.–May 1990, pp. 26–31.

Describes the influence of trade strife on U.S. Japan relations, focusing on the emergence of trade revisionism, which is described as the belief that the bilateral imbalance in trade between the two countries existed because Japan simply did not play by the same free market rules as the U.S. It appeared to be capitalist; it dressed like a capitalist, walked like a capitalist, made capitalist goods and money, but actually it was some sort of Confucian duck.

B022. Morita, A. **QUALITY LESSONS FROM THE MASTER.** *Business and Society Review*, No. 69, Spring 1989, pp. 30–33.

The chairman of Sony Corporation argues that it is not feasible for the United States to try to correct an imbalance of trade in goods with high added value by manipulating the exchange rate alone. The only possible corrective is a raising of the standard quality of the goods being produced.

B023. Nanto, D.K. **EASTERN EUROPE AND JAPAN–U.S. ECONOMIC RELATIONS.** *Journal of Northeast Asian Studies*, Vol. 9, Spring 1990, pp. 3–21.

Japan will probably benefit from changes in Eastern Europe. The government has offered a $1.9 billion assistance package to Hungary and Poland, its businesses are cautiously concluding joint ventures and investments there, and it is cooperating with Europe and the United States in reconstruction efforts. The effects on Japan–U.S. relations will be small though positive, since cooperative efforts of aid and in relaxing export controls seem to outweigh risks of confrontation.

B024. Niskanen, W.A. **THE BULLY OF WORLD TRADE.** *Orbis*, Vol. 33, Fall 1989, pp. 531–538.

Claims that the U.S. government now says, in effect, that any practice perceived to harm U.S. interests is unfair, whether or not it is consistent with international trade rules or is similar to practices found in the United States and other countries. By so defining unfair trade, the U.S. government feels free to demand that other governments change their domestic laws, regulations, and business practices to serve American desires. If they fail to do so, Super 301 legislation allows the U.S. government to back up its demand by threatening foreign governments with punitive U.S. tariffs on their countries' products.

B025. Noland, M. **PROSPECTIVE CHANGES IN JAPAN'S TRADE PATTERN.** *Japan and the World Economy*, Vol. 2, No. 3, 1990, pp. 211–238.

This paper generates projections of Japan's trade pattern for the year 2000. Within the manufacturing sector there is a shift toward more human capital intensive exports. There is also an increase in intra-industry trade, though the degree of intra-industry trade remains low.

B026. Oka, T. **JAPAN'S NEXT BIG CHANGE.** *World Monitor*, Vol. 2, Dec. 1989, pp. 30–39.

Claims that the closed-door economy the Japan bashers love to hate is already opening up faster than Western critics realize. Says that even if drastic short-term measures may be unavoidable to erase the U.S.–Japan trade gap, negotiators must not lose sight of the two countries' common interests and goals.

B027. Peters, M.E. **FREE TRADE AREA AGREEMENTS AS THE ECONOMIC AND LEGAL SOLUTION TO BILATERAL TRADE RELATIONSHIPS: THE CASE OF JAPAN.** *Columbia Journal of Transnational Law*, Vol. 28, 1990, pp. 499–530.

Note examines the basic framework of a Free Trade Area (FTA) with reference to U.S. agreements with Israel and Canada. Concludes that though the United States and Japan should consider a U.S.–Japan FTA as a bilateral alternative, the inability to incorporate market access reforms in FTA negotiations might impede the process and ultimately result in the failure of an FTA to mitigate trade tensions.

B028. Punke, M.W. **STRUCTURAL IMPEDIMENTS TO UNITED STATES–JAPANESE TRADE: THE COLLISION OF CULTURE AND LAW.** *Cornell International Law Journal*, Vol. 23, Winter 1990, pp. 55–81.

Comment argues that the United States and Japan have failed to improve their trade relations because they have failed to effectively recognize and contend with the major source of trade tensions: cultural trade barriers....Advocates the establishment of a standing, bilateral trade arbitration panel to resolve various disputes.

B029. Rehbein, R.E. **THE JAPAN–SOVIET FAR EAST TRADE RELATIONSHIP: A CASE OF THE CAUTIOUS BUYER AND THE OVERCONFIDENT SELLER.** *Journal of Northeast Asian Studies*, Vol. 8, Summer 1989, pp. 38–64.

Discusses what would appear to be a natural fit between the two countries' needs and abilities, explores the extensive joint Siberian development projects of the 1960s and 1970s,....outlines Japanese desires to accrue political advantages from its trade with the Soviet Union, and predicts the inability of Gorbachev's economic reforms to truly expand Japanese–Soviet trade.

B030. Sinha, Radha. **ARE EC–JAPAN–U.S. TRADE RELATIONS AT THE CROSSROADS?** *Intereconomics*, Vol. 25, Sept.–Oct. 1990, pp. 29–237.

The Uruguay Round negotiations are currently passing through a critical phase after four years of strenuous bargaining. The ultimate success of the negotiations largely depends on the attitudes of the U.S.A. the EC and Japan. What are the main contentious issues between these three and how are their trade relations likely to develop in future?

B031. Stelzer, I.M. **HOW TO SAVE FREE TRADE—AND STILL TRADE WITH JAPAN.** *Commentary*, Vol. 90, July 1990, pp. 15–21.

Reviews the recent history of U.S.–Japan trade relations within the rubric of free trade versus protectionism trade policy positions. Rejects both arguments in their purist form. Concludes that so we are left with the middle ground between pure, unilateral free trade and protectionism—the policy of reciprocity which underlies GATT and which has encouraged an almost ten-fold increase in world trade since 1950.

B032. Stern, R.M. (Ed.) **TRADE AND INVESTMENT RELATIONS AMONG THE UNITED STATES, CANADA AND JAPAN.** Univ. of Chicago Press, 1990, ISBN 0-226-77317-5.

B033. Stokes, B. **SWITCHING SIDES.** *National Journal*, Vol. 22, Nov. 24, 1990, pp. 2862–2865.

In Washington's close-knit community of trade experts, lobbyists are up in arms about accusations that they have sold out to foreign—mainly Japanese—interests. But Congress isn't considered likely to lock the revolving door.

B034. **SYMPOSIUM—THE MERGER POLICY DEBATE CONTINUES: RESPONSES TO THE BIGNESS MYSTIQUE.** *Northwestern Journal of International Law & Business*, Vol. 9, Winter 1989, pp. 588–632.

Response to an earlier article by Walter Adams and James W. Brock. Contents—Does exposure to international trade justify relaxed antitrust treatment of mergers? by W.J. Adams. Merger policy and industrial policy, by K. Cowling. The problem of mergers, by H.W. deJong. Japan and the bigness mystique, by G.R. Saxonhouse. The bigness mystique and the merger policy debate: a comment from West Germany, by I.L.O. Schmidt.

B035. Thurwachter, T. **JAPAN IN CHINA: THE GUANGDONG EXAMPLE.** *China Business Review*, Vol. 17, Jan.–Feb. 1990, pp. 7–10,12–17.

Analyzes the levels and composition of Sino-Japanese trade, contrasting this with the data for U.S. trade with China. From 1984–88, Japan exported more than three times as much to China as did the United States: $57 billion versus $18.5 billion. And while Japan has maintained a multi-billion dollar trade surplus with China over this period, the U.S. trade deficit with China has grown from less than $400 million to 4.2 billion.

B036. Tsurumi, Y. **U.S.–JAPANESE RELATIONS: FROM BRINKMANSHIP TO STATESMANSHIP.** *World Policy Journal*, Vol. 7, Winter 1989–90, pp. 1–33.

B037. **U.S. CONGRESS. HOUSE. COMMITTEE ON ENERGY AND COMMERCE. SUBCOMMITTEE ON COMMERCE, CONSUMER PROTECTION AND COMPETITIVENESS.**

Foreign trade barriers. Hearing, 101st Congress, 2nd session. Apr. 24, 1990, Washington, G.P.O., 1990, p. 112. Serial no. 101–132.

B038. **U.S. CONGRESS. HOUSE. COMMITTEE ON ENERGY AND COMMERCE. SUBCOMMITTEE ON COMMERCE, CONSUMER PROTECTION, AND COMPETITIVENESS.**

U.S. trade relations with Japan. Hearing, 101st Congress, 2nd session. May 10, 1990, Washington, G.P.O., 1990, p. 34. Serial no. 101–150. Hears testimony from Carla Hills, the U.S. Trade Representative, on Japanese trade practices and continuing trade negotiations.

B039. **U.S. CONGRESS. HOUSE. COMMITTEE ON FOREIGN AFFAIRS. SUBCOMMITTEE ON ASIAN AND PACIFIC AFFAIRS.**

United States–Japan relations: causes of economic imbalances. Hearing before the Subcommittees on Asian and Pacific Affairs and on International Economic Policy and Trade of the Committee on Foreign Affairs, House of Representatives, 100th Congress, 2nd session. Sept. 14, 1988, Washington, G.P.O., 1989, p. 56.

B040. **U.S. CONGRESS. HOUSE. COMMITTEE ON FOREIGN AFFAIRS. SUBCOMMITTEE ON ASIAN AND PACIFIC AFFAIRS.**

United States–Japan relations: the impact of negotiated market openings. Hearings before the Subcommittees on Asian and Pacific Affairs and on International Economic Policy and Trade of the Committee on Foreign Affairs, House of Representatives, 100th Congress, 2nd session, Washington, G.P.O., 1989, p. 306. Hearings held Sept. 27–28 and Oct. 13, 1988. Hearings to evaluate one of the principal methods by which the Reagan Administration has sought to address United States–Japanese economic tensions; that is negotiated market openings on a sector-by-sector basis.

B041. **U.S. CONGRESS. HOUSE. COMMITTEE ON WAYS AND MEANS. SUBCOMMITTEE ON TRADE.**

USTR identification of priority practices and countries under Super 301 and Special 301 provisions of the Omnibus Trade and Competitiveness Act of 1988. Hearing, 101st Congress, 1st session. June 8, 1989. Washington, G.P.O., 1989, p. 138. Serial no. 101–28.

B042. **U.S. CONGRESS. JOINT ECONOMIC COMMITTEE.**
The Japanese market: how open is it? Hearing, 101st Congress, 1st session. Oct. 11, 1989, Washington, G.P.O., 1990, p. 83. (Hearing, Senate, 101st Congress, 1st session, S. Hrg. 101–531). Three experts on Japanese trade: Mr. Raymond Ahearn is a Specialist in Trade Relations at the Congressional Research Service. Mr. Robert Lawrence is a senior fellow at the Brookings Institution, and Mr. Clyde Prestowitz is a senior associate at the Carnegie Endowment for International Peace.

B043. **U.S. CONGRESS. SENATE. COMMITTEE ON FINANCE. SUBCOMMITTEE ON INTERNATIONAL TRADE.**
Japanese trade barriers to forest products. Hearing, 101st Congress, 1st session, June 22, 1989, Washington, G.P.O., 1990, p. 39. (Hearing, Senate, 101st Congress, 1st session, S. Hrg. 101–526, Pt. 1).

B044. **U.S. CONGRESS. SENATE. COMMITTEE ON FINANCE. SUBCOMMITTEE ON INTERNATIONAL TRADE.**
Japanese trade barriers to forest products. Hearing, 101st Congress, 2nd session. Feb. 26, 1990. Washington, G.P.O., 1990, p. 26. (Hearing, 101st Congress, 2nd session, S. Hrg. 101–526, Pt. 2).

B045. **U.S. CONGRESS. SENATE. COMMITTEE ON FINANCE. SUBCOMMITTEE ON INTERNATIONAL TRADE.**
Trade between Montana and the Pacific Rim. Hearing, 101st Congress, 1st session, Dec. 8, 1989, Washington, G.P.O., 1990, p. 61. (Hearing, 101st Congress, 1st session, S. Hrg. 101–542). Hearing held in Billings, MT.

B046. **U.S. CONGRESS. SENATE. COMMITTEE ON FINANCE SUBCOMMITTEE ON INTERNATIONAL TRADE.**
United States–Japan Structural Impediments Initiative (SII). Hearing, 101st Congress, 1st session, July 20, 1989, Washington, G.P.O., 1990, p. 37. (Hearing, 101st Congress, 1st session, S. Hrg. 101–594, Pt. 1)

B047. **U.S. CONGRESS. SENATE. COMMITTEE ON FINANCE. SUBCOMMITTEE ON INTERNATIONAL TRADE.**
United States–Japan Structural Impediments Initiative (SII). Hearing, 101st Congress, 2nd session. Part 3 of 3. Mar. 5, 1990, Washington, G.P.O., 1990, p. 114. (Hearing, 101st Senate, 2nd session, S. Hrg. 101–594, pt. 3). Includes reprint of a Dept. of Commerce survey (Oct. 1989) comparing prices of over 100 products sold in both the U.S. and Japan.

B048. **U.S. CONGRESS. SENATE. COMMITTEE ON FINANCE. SUBCOMMITTEE ON INTERNATIONAL TRADE.**
United States–Japan Structural Impediments Initiative (SII). Hearing, 101st Congress, 1st session. Part 2 of 3, Nov. 6–7, 1989, Washington, G.P.O., 1990, p. 239. (Hearing, 101st Senate, 1st session, S. Hrg. 101–594, Pt. 2).

B049. **U.S. CONGRESS. SENATE. COMMITTEE ON SMALL BUSINESS. SUBCOMMITTEE ON INNOVATION TECHNOLOGY AND PRODUCTIVITY.**

United States/Japan auto parts trade. Hearing, 101st Congress, 1st session, Apr. 20, 1990, Washington, G.P.O., 1990, p. 69. (Hearing, Senate, 101st Congress, 1st session, S. Hrg, 101–856).

B050. **U.S. INTERNATIONAL TRADE ADMINISTRATION.** Office of Forest Products and Domestic Construction. Basic Industries Sector. The Japanese solid wood products market: profile and outlook. Washington, The Administration, 1989, p. 194.

Contents—Executive summary. Impediments to increased solid wood products exports to Japan. Japanese consumption of forest products. Japan's forest resources. Japan's wood based industries. Barriers to trade. International trade.

B051. van Wolferen, K. **THE JAPAN PROBLEM REVISITED.** *Foreign Affairs*, Vol. 69, Fall 1990, pp. 42—55.

Addresses the potential dangers of continuing trade-related conflicts between Japan and the U.S. Claims that efforts such as the SII (Structural Impediments Initiative), aimed at changing the way Japanese organizations do business, are bound to fail in the long run. Calls for a new institutional framework, such as an overhauled GATT, that could bring international discipline to the global free trade system.

B052. Yamamoto, S. **JAPAN'S TRADE LEAD: BLAME PROFIT-HUNGRY AMERICAN FIRMS.** *Brookings Review*, Vol. 8, Winter 1989–90, pp. 14–18.

Claims that in contrast to Japanese companies, American firms have tended to withdraw from manufacturing products that they judge to have low operating profits, and they have engaged in streamlining operations that lead to mergers, plant closings, and layoffs. These policies may raise profits but at the cost of reduced output and employment. Urges the U.S. to lower interest rates, allow the value of the dollar to fall, and emphasize long-term profits.

C. SECURITY; DEFENSE; MILITARY AFFAIRS

C001. Agres, T. **FSX DEAL POLARIZES OPINIONS OF TRADE IN U.S. AND JAPAN.** *Research and Development*, Vol. 31, May 1989, pp 36–37, 40, 42.

The agreement to codevelop Japan's next-generation fighter jet has polarized opinion in both the U.S. and Japan. As if symbolic, the issue also has put the U.S. Defense and Commerce departments on opposite sides of the technology export table.

C002. Akaha, T. **JAPAN'S SECURITY POLICY AFTER US HEGEMONY.** *Millennium*, Vol. 18, Winter 1989, pp 435–454.

This article examines the impact of the post-hegemonic proposition on the security debate in Japan, with an emphasis on the cornerstone of Japan's security policy: its ties with the US.

C003. **ARMING OUR ALLIES: COOPERATION AND COMPETITION IN DEFENSE TECHNOLOGY.** Washington: U.S. Office of Technology Assessment, G.P.O., 1990, 113 pp.

Contents:—Interdependence in defense technology.—Implications and issues for Congress.—European policies in perspective.—Emergence of Transpacific collaboration: the case of Japan.—Commercial implications of international collaboration.

C004. Auer, J.E. **THE U.S.-JAPAN FSX AGREEMENT: COOPERATION OR CONFRONTATION IN HIGH TECHNOLOGY.** *Business in the Contemporary World*, Vol. 2, Summer 1990, pp 105–112.

An account of the tumultuous process leading to the U.S.-Japan agreement of FSX co-development from one of the leading negotiators.

C005. Bean, R.M. **COOPERATIVE SECURITY IN NORTHEAST ASIA.** Washington, National Defense University, G.P.O., 1990, p. 198.

Contents—The changing security environment. The emerging triangle: China–Japan–South Korea. Toward a stronger triangle. Security threat and response. The triangle and the United States.

C006. Brogan, P. **LOSERS IN BATTLE OVER FSX FIND REASON TO CHEER.** *Legal Times*, Vol. 11, May 22, 1989, pp 2, 14–15.

Opponents of the FSX fighter plane lost the battle when the Senate narrowly approved an administration plan to build the jet with Japan, but critics of the agreement contend they also scored a partial victory: economic interests, they say, will no longer take a back seat to defense concerns.

C007. Chen, K.T. **THE STATE OF JAPAN'S MILITARY ART.** *IEEE Spectrum*, Vol. 26, Sept. 1989, pp 28–33.

The FSX fighter jet exemplifies how the world's third-largest defense spender benefits from technology transfer programs from the United States.

C008. Cheney, R.B. **TO REMAIN IN ASIA: A FIRM U.S. DEFENSE COMMITMENT.** *Speaking of Japan*, Vol. 11, June 1990, pp 1–7.

Presents the text of the speech of the U.S. Secretary of Defense, Richard B. Cheney, to the Japan National Press Club, in Tokyo, February 23, 1990

C009. Cheung, T.M. **A YEN FOR ARMS: JAPAN DEFENCE INDUSTRY'S RAPID GROWTH BEGINS TO SLOW.** *Far Eastern Economic Review*, Vol. 147, Feb 22, 1990, pp 58–60, 62.

Japan's defence industry has thrived, and is thriving. But for all the talk of Japanese rearmament, the days of rapid growth for Japan's military-industrial-bureaucratic complex are over for now.

C010. Chinworth, M.W. **INDUSTRY AND GOVERNMENT IN JAPANESE DEFENSE PROCUREMENT: THE CASE OF THE PATRIOT MISSILE SYSTEM.** *Comparative Strategy*, Vol. 9, No. 3, 1990, pp. 195–244.

Numerous players and considerations are involved in the procurement of weapons systems by the Japan Defense Agency. Business and government in Japan interact in both formal and informal ways with long-term objectives in mind. Government and business have embarked on a policy of utilizing licensed production and coproduction programs to develop a full range of indigenous system.

C011. Corning, G.P. **U.S.–JAPAN SECURITY COOPERATION IN THE 1990s.** *Asian Survey*, Vol. 29, Mar. 1989, pp. 268–286.

A new effort to deal constructively with the trade and security dimensions of U.S.–Japan relations should be high on the foreign policy agenda of the Bush administration. To demonstrate the feasibility and importance of such cooperation, this article addresses Japanese and American perspectives on Japan's security role as well as the advantages and disadvantages of the available options in bilateral security policy.

C012. Ebata, K. **DOGFIGHT OVER THE PACIFIC.** *Tokyo Business Today*, Apr. 1989, pp. 14–19.

Continuing debate over the FSX project envisaged by Japan has uncovered new strains in its relationship with the U.S. Is Japan capable of developing advanced defense-oriented aircraft without substantial U.S. support? And does the project posse a serious threat to U.S. aerospace dominance?

C013. Ennis, P. **INSIDE THE PENTAGON-COMMERCE TURF WAR.** *Tokyo Business Today*, Vol. 57, Oct. 1989, pp. 22–26.

Discusses the contentious debate over U.S. plans participate in Japan's FSX jet fighter program. Focuses on the role that the differing interests of the Dept. of Defense and the Dept. of Commerce had in bringing the debate over the jet fighter to a head.

C014. Ennis, P. **TECHNOLOGY TRANSFERS ARE NOW FLOWING BOTH WAYS.** *Tokyo Business Today*, Vol. 57, Sept. 1989, pp. 24–27.

In the past, Japan relied almost exclusively on American technology for new manufacturing techniques. There are now signs that the relationship has become more equitable.

C015. **FSX** (Part 1 of II). Prepared by the American Forces Information Service. [Washington]: Current News Analysis and Research Service, 1989, 40 pp.
A collection of editorials and newspaper articles.

C016. **FSX : Part II**. Prepared by the American Forces Information Service. [Washington]: Current News Analysis and Research Service, 1989, 42 pp.
A collection of editorials and newspaper articles.

C017. Greenwald, J. **FRIEND OR FOE?** *Time*, Vol. 133, Apr. 24, 1989, pp. 44–45.
The FSX becomes a symbol of mounting strain between the U.S. and Japan.

C018. Griffin, T.P. and Farr, C.M. **THE FSX DEBATE: IMPLICATIONS FOR FUTURE U.S. INTERNATIONAL ARMAMENTS PROGRAMS.** *Program Manager*, Vol. 18, July–Aug. 1989, pp. 2–13.
A great debate has risen over the joint program between the United States and Japan to develop the next-generation fighter aircraft for the Japanese Air Self-Defense....The focus of the debate centers on issues such as protection of technology, trade balances and international security relationships...Of greater significance is the implication such review holds for the future of U.S. international cooperative programs.

C019. Harrison, S.S. and Prestowitz, C.V., Jr. **PACIFIC AGENDA: DEFENSE OR ECONOMICS?** *Foreign Policy*, No. 79, summer, 1990, pp. 56–76.
Asserts that even before the Berlin Wall fell the fundamental challenge facing the U.S. was not the Soviet threat but the danger of economic insolvency, reflected in budget deficits, an eroding industrial base, and the growing American inability to compete with newly formidable economic rivals, especially Japan, South Korea, and Taiwan. Argues that the United States should strengthen its leverage and expand its room to maneuver by negotiating a large-scale mutual reduction of Soviet and American forces in the Pacific. Ironically, in a more relaxed security environment, greater U.S. leverage can lead to a moderation rather than an increase in trade frictions. Freed from the necessity to pretend that the U.S. and East Asian economic systems are the same as a rationale for the alliances, the United States could acknowledge the reality of systemic differences and deal with them in a more pragmatic and flexible manner.

C020. Hayes, T.C. **FSX: ICING ON THE CAKE FOR GENERAL DYNAMICS.** *New York Times*, May 2, 1989, D1,D6.
The business that General Dynamics is expected to get from the joint FSX fighter project of the United States and Japan, which will be based on the F-16, will be mere icing on the corporate profits cake, not something that will make or break the company.

C021. **HENRY S. ROWEN ON U.S.–JAPAN DEFENSE RELATIONS IN A NEW GLOBAL ORDER.** *Japan Economic Survey*, Vol. 14, Aug. 1990, pp. 6–10.
The reform movement in Eastern Europe and recent improvements in U.S.—Soviet relations have raised questions on both sides of the Pacific

about the impact of these developments on East Asian society. In a recent conversation with JES editor Barbara Wanner, Henry S. Rowen, assistant secretary of defense for international security affairs, examines how the transition to a new global order will affect U.S.–Japan defense cooperation.

C022. Ito, K. **TRANS-PACIFIC ANGER.** *Foreign Policy,* Vol. 78, spring 1990, pp. 131–152.

Discusses and examines the rising antagonism between Japan and the U.S. Argues that a bilateral economic council, a trade court, and closer military cooperation are necessary because without such new coordinating systems, U.S.–Japanese relations will worsen steadily in the coming years. A nationalistic, mean-spirited rivalry between the two nations...will undoubtedly strengthen the hands of the New Asianists in Japan. The result could be the creation of a Japanese economic sphere of influence in the Asia–Pacific region and the gradual weakening of the U.S.–Japanese alliance.

C023. **JAPAN'S DEFENSE INDUSTRY.** Washington: Japan Economic Institute, 1990, 14 pp.

C024. **JAPAN'S FSX: WHAT'S BEHIND THE CONTROVERSY.** *Estimate,* Vol. 1, Feb. 24–Mar. 9, 1989, pp. 5–8.

The current impasse within the U.S. Administration which has led to a delay in the implementation of the Japanese FSX (Fighter Support Experimental) project is the result of a fundamental debate within the U.S. policy community over issues of technology transfer.

C025. Johnson, P. **INTERNATIONAL IMPROPRIETIES.** *American Enterprise,* Vol. 1, Jan.–Feb. 1990, pp. 34–39.

Examines the role of the media in the changing impact of political scandals of public life. Looking at the coverage of recent American, British, French, and Japanese scandals, the author finds that the importance of national characteristics in determining the relative seriousness of different kinds of scandals has been diminishing. The practices and interests of the media are steadily taking on a transnational flavor.

C026. Kearns, K.L. **AFTER FSX: A NEW APPROACH TO U.S.–JAPAN RELATIONS.** *Foreign Service Journal,* Vol. 66, Dec. 1989, pp. 43–48.

The United States must make a new effort on the national level to formulate a coherent policy toward Japan, one that covers the many facets of the relationship....The FSX became a watershed in relations between the U.S. and Japan.

C027. Kohno. M. **JAPANESE DEFENSE POLICY-MAKING: THE FSX SELECTION, 1985–1987.** *Asian Survey,* Vol. 29, May 1989, pp. 457–479.

Japanese policy makers face more immediate and formidable pressure from Washington than from the international political opposition. A systematic analysis is necessary to understand (1) how the Americans express their own interests and interfere with the autonomy of Japanese decision-making (2) why and to what extent the Japanese are sensitive or vulnerable to American pressure; and (3) how, if at all, Japan's final decisions reflect American interests. In an attempt to address these questions, this article examines as a case study the recent selection of the next-generation fighter support (jiki shien sentoki) of the Japanese Air Self-Defense Force (ASDF), usually referred to as the FSX.

C028. Kusumi, E. **RIJUSENTAI (JAPANESE MARINE CORPS.).** *Marine Corps Gazette,* Vol. 73, Sept. 1989, pp. 64–70.

Japanese Naval Officer assigned to that nation's Marine Corps during the Second World War, discusses Marine Corps operations and Japanese naval operations.

C029. Marshall, P.G. **SHOULD THE U.S. REDUCE ITS PACIFIC FORCES?** Washington: *Congressional Quarterly,* 1990, pp 222–235.

Contents.—U.S. Pacific policy.—Soviet Pacific strategy.—Stronger role for Japan?—Korea: potential hot spot.—Future of Philippine bases.—Looking ahead.

C030. Matsukane, H. **JAPAN AND SECURITY OF THE SEA LANES.** Global Affairs, Vol. 4, spring 1989, pp. 49–64.

In view of the heightened Soviet military threat in the Far East, it is Japan's responsibility to systematically improve the quality and quantity of its ground, maritime, and air forces.

C031. Mecham, M. **TECHNOLOGY CONCERNS DELAY APPROVAL OF FSX AGREEMENT.** *Aviation Week and Space Technology,* Vol. 130, Feb. 20, 1989, pp. 16–17.

U.S. technology transfer policy for development of the airframe of Japan's Fighter Support-Experimental (FSX) aircraft....the FSX dispute blends trade and national security issues.

C032. Menon, R. and Abele, D. **SECURITY DIMENSIONS OF SOVIET TERRITORIAL DISPUTES WITH CHINA AND JAPAN.** *Journal of Northeast Asian Studies,* Vol. 8, spring 1989, pp. 3–19.

The advent of Mikhail Gorbachev's New Thinking has produced a Soviet strategy toward East Asia that seeks a detente with China and Japan. An essential part of this task involves settling the territorial disputes that both countries have with the USSR. Present negotiations on the Sino-Soviet border have produced compromises, yet differences remain. Intractable positions by Japan and the USSR on the Northern Territories issue have resulted in a standstill.....This article analyzes the strategic-military choices that Soviet leaders will have to make as they address the territorial disputes.

C033. Namatame, O. **THE FSX: SOURCE OF FRICTION AND COOPERATION.** *World and I,* Vol. 4, July 1989, pp. 141–145.

The joint U.S.–Japanese development of a controversial new fighter aircraft for Japan will be successful only if both nations deal with it within the framework of greater burden-sharing.

C034. **THE NAVAL BALANCE 1990.** *Naval Forces,* Vol. 11, No. 11., 1990, whole issue pp. 1–115.

Partial contents—The U.S. Navy: global commitments, fewer dollars, greater uncertainty, by S.C. Truver. East European Navies: revolutionary change, by M. Vego. The Soviet Navy under Gorbachev: future conditional?

by G. Till. African Navies: diminutive growth, by J. Ukubiala. Japan's maritime self defence force, by G.A. Rubinstein and J. O'Connell.

C035. Niksch, L.A. **BURDEN SHARING AND POWER SHARING.** *Congressional Research Service Review*, Vol. 10, July 1989, pp. 19–20.

The United States is engaged in negotiations with Japan over the division of responsibilities and financial costs for defenses and other security-related policies. This issue emerged because of new defense and strategic considerations following the 1979 Soviet invasion of Afghanistan. Subsequent economic disputes between Japan and the United States make future agreement on equitable burden sharing arrangements more complex.

C036. Painter, F.C. **FSX—PORTRAIT OF A DILEMMA.** *Defense Electronics*, Vol. 21, May 1989, pp. 40–41,43.

Failure of the joint FSX deal could open the door for Japan to go it alone.

C037. Richards, E. **FSX BECOMES SYMBOL OF A NEW AGE.** *Washington Post*, Mar. 27, 1989, A1,A12.

The accord reached last fall provided a broad framework for transfers of technology but did not spell out the details.

C038. **THE RISING SON: JAPAN'S NEW EMPEROR, A MAN OF THE PEOPLE, ACCEDES TO THE THRONE; HIROTO'S DEATH MAY STIR DEBATE ANEW OVER ROLE OF THE MONARCH IN SOCIETY.** *Wall Street Journal*, Jan. 9, 1989, A1,A10.

Profiles Japan's new Emperor Akihito and discusses his likely role in Japanese society.

C039. Robinson, T.W. (Ed.) **ASIAN SECURITY.** Lanham: University Press of America, Inc., ISBN 0-8447-3723-2, 300 pp.

C040. Shinji, O. **THE FSX CONTROVERSY REVIVED.** *Japan Quarterly*, Vol. 36, Oct.–Dec. 1989, pp. 433–443.

The wrenching political dispute over development of the Japanese Air Self-Defense Force's next-generation support fighter (FSX) is an example with serious ramifications for the Japanese. Why did the United States reopen negotiations on a joint development agreement that the Japanese considered closed? And how did the Japanese people react to this unprecedented American demand to fundamentally change the substance of an agreement that had already been officially concluded?

C041. Sneider, D. **FSX, IT'S A GOOD DEAL FOR AMERICAN AND JAPAN.** *Christian Science Monitor*, Feb. 23, 1989, p. 19.

If the opponents are successful in derailing the deal, it will only serve the interests of those Japanese most intent on building a world-class aerospace industry.

C042. Sneider, D. **FSX NEGOTIATIONS: THE INSIDE VIEW.** *Christian Science Monitor*, June 14, 1989, p. 6.

A close look at the FSX decision-making process reveals a story of bureaucratic conflict; of the difficulties of reaching bilateral agreements when governments are divided.

C043. Steinhoff, P.G. **HIJACKERS, BOMBERS, AND BANK ROBBERS: MANAGERIAL STYLE IN THE JAPANESE RED ARMY.** *Journal of Asian Studies*, Vol. 48, Nov. 1989, pp. 724–740.

This study examines the organizational development of Sekigun (Red Army), a group whose members came out of the mainstream of Japanese youth but placed themselves in conflict with both state and society....The name Sekigun encompasses three related groups that shared a particular ideological vision: the original group began as the Sekigunha (Red Army Faction); a remnant of the original Sekigun to become Rengo Sekigun (United Red Army). The last group, known variously as Arabu Sekigun (Arab Red Army) and Nihon Sekigun (Japanese Red Army), remains active today.

C044. Stokes, B. **BEAT 'EM OR JOIN 'EM.** *National Journal*, Vol. 21, Feb, 25, 1989, pp. 459–464.

The flap over U.S. plans to coproduce a tactical fighter plane with Japan is spotlighting a division in the U.S. trade community between those who favor collaborating with Japan and those who want confrontation.

C045. Tajiri, T. **JAPAN AND MARITIME DISARMAMENT.** *Global Affairs*, Vol. 5, summer–fall 1990, pp. 94–113.

The Soviet Union and the United States, as architects of the new world, are prepared to negotiate the creation of a new security environment...Given the manifest readiness for disarmament and the reduction of international tension, Mikhail Gorbachev has introduced proposals for a reduction in naval forces.

C046. Takagi, J. and Nishio, B. **JAPAN'S FAKE PLUTONIUM SHORTAGE.** *Bulletin of the Atomic Scientists*, Vol. 46, Oct. 1990, pp. 34–38.

Questions Japan's alleged need for plutonium and discusses international concern for Japan's plans to transport the material from mines in France and Britain. Suggests there is a threat of nuclear terrorism.

C047. Towell, P. **U.S.–JAPAN FIGHTER-JET DEAL IS CLEARED FOR TAKEOFF.** *Congressional Quarterly Weekly Report*, Vol. 47, May 20, 1989, pp. 1189–1199.

In the wake of the Senate's vote on the FSX deal, wide-ranging congressional anger lingers.

C048. Towell, P. **U.S.–JAPANESE WARPLANE DEAL RAISES A WELTER OF ISSUES.** *Congressional Quarterly Weekly Report*, Vol. 47, Mar. 11, 1989, pp. 535–537.

Sets forth the arguments of both the opponents and the proponents of the proposal for U.S.–Japanese codevelopment of the new FSX fighter aircraft.

C049. **U.S. CONGRESS. HOUSE. COMMITTEE ON ARMED SERVICES. INVESTIGATIONS SUBCOMMITTEE.**

The proposed FSX agreement with Japan. Hearings, 101st Congress, 1st session. May 4 and 16, 1989, Washington, G.P.O., 1990, p. 142. At the head of title: H.A.S.C. no. 101–38. The FSX fighter, the proposal to sell F-16 technology to the Japanese.

C050. **U.S. CONGRESS. HOUSE. COMMITTEE ON BANKING, FINANCE AND URBAN AFFAIRS. SUBCOMMITTEE ON ECONOMIC STABILIZATION.**
Proposed joint development of the FSX fighter with Japan. Hearings, 101st Congress, 1st session. Washington, G.P.O., 1989, p. 274. Serial no. 101–20. Hearings held Apr. 18 and May 5, 1989.

C051. **U.S. CONGRESS. HOUSE. COMMITTEE ON ENERGY AND COMMERCE. SUBCOMMITTEE ON COMMERCE, CONSUMER PROTECTION, AND COMPETITIVENESS.**
FSX codevelopment project. Hearing, 100th Congress, 1st session. Feb. 23, 1989, Washington, G.P.O., 1989, p. 95. Serial no. 101–5.

C052. **U.S. CONGRESS. HOUSE. COMMITTEE ON FOREIGN AFFAIRS.**
Codevelopment and coproduction of the FSX weapon system; report together with minority views to accompany S.J. Res. 113 including cost estimate of the Congressional Budget Office. (Washington, G.P.O.) 1989, p. 11 (Report, House, 101st Congress, 1st session, no. 101–71).

C053. **U.S. CONGRESS. HOUSE. COMMITTEE ON FOREIGN AFFAIRS. SUBCOMMITTEE ON ARMS CONTROL, INTERNATIONAL SECURITY AND SCIENCE.**
United States–Japanese security cooperation and the FSX agreement. Hearings and markup before the Committee on Foreign Affairs and its Subcommittees on Arms Control, International Security and Science, on Asian and Pacific Affairs, and on International Economic Policy and Trade, House of Representatives, 101st Congress, 1st session on S.J. Res. 113. Washington, G.P.O., 1989, p. 490. Hearings held Apr. 13–May 23, 1989. The controversy which appears to have erupted over the proposed FSX deal between the United States and Japan.

C054. **U.S. CONGRESS. HOUSE. COMMITTEE ON SCIENCE, SPACE, AND TECHNOLOGY. SUBCOMMITTEE ON INVESTIGATIONS AND OVERSIGHT.**
FSX. Hearings before the Subcommittee on Investigations and Oversight and the Subcommittee on International Scientific Cooperation and the Subcommittee on Transportation, Aviation and Materials of the Committee on Science, Space, and Technology, U.S. House of, l Representatives, Washington, G.P.O., 1989, p. 443. Serial no. 62. Hearing held Apr. 6; May 11, 1989.

C055. **U.S. CONGRESS. HOUSE. JOINT ECONOMIC COMMITTEE.**
Japan's economic challenge; study papers submitted to the Joint Economic Committee, Congress of the United States. Washington, G.P.O., 1990, p. 498. (Print, Senate, 101st Congress, 2nd session, joint committee print 5. Prt. 101–121). The current study examines Japan's emergence as an economic superpower. In order to understand this nation's impressive performance and growing global role, there are assessments of its policies, structure, and domestic and international trends. Partial contents—Framework of economic policy. Government and business. Balance and investment. Human resources. Science and technology. National security and foreign aid. International economic relations.

C056. **U.S. CONGRESS. SENATE. COMMITTEE ON ARMED SERVICES. SUBCOMMITTEE ON DEFENSE INDUSTRY AND TECHNOLOGY.**
Implications of the FSX aircraft agreement between the United States and Japan. Hearings, 101st Congress, 1st session. Washington, G.P.O., 1989, p. 189. (Hearings. Senate, 101st Congress, 1st session, S. Hrg. 101–324). Hearings held Mar. 10 and May 9, 1989.

C057. **U.S. GENERAL ACCOUNTING OFFICE.**
U.S.–Japan burden sharing: Japan has increased its contributions but could do more; report to the Chairman, Committee on Armed Services, House of Representatives. Aug. 15, 1989, Washington, G.A.O., 1989, p. 54.

C058. **U.S. GENERAL ACCOUNTING OFFICE.**
U.S.–Japan burden sharing: Japan has increased its contributions but could do more; report to the Chairman, Committee on Armed Services, House of Representatives. Aug. 15, 1989, Washington, G.A.O., 1989, p. 54. Finds that Japan has made steady progress in strengthening its defense capabilities during the last 4 years, after significantly underfunding its defense program during 1980–85. According to U.S. military officials, the current Japanese defense program, if fully funded, will provide Japan with the minimum capability necessary to meet most of this defense responsibilities by 1991, including sea lane protection.

C059. **U.S. GENERAL ACCOUNTING OFFICE.**
U.S.–Japan codevelopment: review of the FSX program; briefing report to congressional requesters. Feb. 6, 1990, Washington, G.A.O., 1990, p. 49.

C060. **U.S. GENERAL ACCOUNTING OFFICE.**
U.S.–Japan FSX Codevelopment Program; statement of Frank C. Conahan, Assistant Comptroller General, National Security and International Relations Division. May 16, 1989, Washington, G.A.O., 1989, p. 14. Assessing the government-to-government and commercial licensing agreements, assessing U.S. and Japanese composite and radar technologies and analyzing cost data.

C061. **U.S. GENERAL ACCOUNTING OFFICE.**
U.S. military aircraft coproduction with Japan; testimony. Feb. 23, 1989, Washington, G.A.O., 1989, p. 11. Discusses the 1982 report on U.S. military aircraft coproduction with Japan.

C062. Vogel, S.K. **JAPANESE HIGH TECHNOLOGY, POLITICS, AND POWER.** Berkeley, CA., Berkeley Roundtable on the International Economy, 1989, p. 124 (Research paper no. 2).
Suggests that Japan is already a military power in the sense that it has the ability to tip the global balance of power—in either direction. For one thing, Japan already spends more on defense than any other country except the United States and the Soviet Union. And if Japan remains the world's No. 3 defense spender, it is bound to become a major regional military power by the turn of the century.

C063. Walker, J.S. **THE DECISION TO USE THE BOMB: A HISTORIOGRAPHICAL UPDATE.** *Diplomatic History,* Vol. 14, winter 1990, pp. 97–114.

C064. Weinraub, G. **U.S. AND JAPANESE AGREE TO PROCEED ON FIGHTER PLANE.** *New York Times,* Apr. 29, 1989, pp. 1,5.

U.S. and Japan agree to build the $7 billion military fighter jet (and) the President is bracing for a fight in Congress.

C065. Zumwalt, E.R., Dornan, R.K. and Bagley, W.H. **THE FSX FLAP.** *Washington Times,* Apr. 4, 1989, F1,F4.

The old adage about two heads are better than one is very apropos to the FSX project.

D. SCIENCE; TECHNOLOGY; ENVIRONMENT

D001. Alic, J.A. **SUPERCONDUCTIVITY: A TEST FOR U.S. TECHNOLOGY POLICY**. *Forum for Applied Research and Public Policy*, Vol. 5, Fall 1990, pp 47–76.

Argues that outdated U.S. technology policy fails to provide commercial firms with adequate support to compete in today's international marketplace. Four additional articles look at technology policy in Japan, Western Europe, the Pacific Rim, and the U.S.

Contents.—Technology policy in Japan, by Leonard H. Lynn.—Technology policy in Europe, by Mark Dodgson and Ian Miles.—Technology policy on the Pacific Rim, by Denis Fred Simon.—Technology policy in the U.S., by Claude E. Barfield.

D002. Berkowitz, B.D. **ENERGIZING THE SPACE LAUNCH INDUSTRY**. *Issues in Science and Technology*, Vol. 6, Winter 1989–90, pp 77–83.

Warns that even though the U.S. commercial launch industry is a vital high technology industry on which future U.S. scientific and military objectives will depend, it is losing its market share to Arianespace, China and Japan.

D003. Brown, H. **COMPETITIVENESS, TECHNOLOGY, AND U.S.-JAPAN RELATIONS**. *Washington Quarterly*, Vol. 13, Summer 1990, pp 85–105.

Harold Brown, former Secretary of Defense, looks at the status of technology, technological innovation, and competitiveness in the United States and Japan. Argues that looking ahead to the next century when the United States and Japan both will be technological superpowers, it is important to begin now to structure and restructure joint ventures, collaborative research, and other forms of science and technology exchange.

D004. Brown, P. **BATTLING OVER YOUR TV**. *Newsday Magazine*, June 24, 1990, pp 10–12, 14–15, 19–20.

Japan and the U.S. are vying to develop a hot new technology called HDTV that will greatly improve the picture. To the winner will go huge profits.

D005. Brownstein, R. **FACING WEST, NERVOUSLY**. *National Journal*, Vol. 21, Oct 28, 1989, pp 2624–2629.

California, Oregon and Washington on the front line of the Pacific Rim, share America's enormous ambivalence about the nation's growing economic links to Asia. Focuses on wood products and the semiconductor industry.

D006. Bylinsky, G. **THE HOTTEST HIGH-TECH COMPANY IN JAPAN.** *Fortune*, Vol. 121, Jan 1, 1990, pp 82–84, 86, 88.

Describes Kyocera Corp. as a maverick company: prototypically Japanese in the way it manages people and manufacturing, decidedly un-Japanese in its emphasis on innovation through highly original research. Here's a Japanese company that doesn't snitch Western high-tech secrets. Instead, Kyocera is a pioneer.

D007. Bylinsky, G. **WHERE JAPAN WILL STRIKE NEXT.** *Fortune*, Vol. 120, Sept. 25, 1989, pp 42–46, 48, 50, 52.

Describes the likely products and services soon to be launched by Japanese companies. Primed with an arsenal of high-tech products from filmless cameras to mid-engine sports cars, they are also preparing to branch out across the globe in services from credit cards to construction. They are confident about their ability to innovate in technology, not just to capitalize on technology borrowed from somebody else.

D008. **CHALLENGE AND OPPORTUNITIES FOR TOMORROW.** Paris: Organization for Economic Cooperation and Development, 1989, 179 pp.

A compendium of the speeches presented at the Seminar marking the 20th Anniversary of the Road Transport Research Program.

Partial contents.—Reflections in the dynamics of industrial societies and on tomorrow's road transport, by Andre Jaumotte.—Major tasks for the future of road transport in Japan, by Masaki Koshi.

D009. **COMPARATIVE LEGAL ASPECTS OF THE ENVIRONMENT FOR INNOVATION IN THE CANADA-U.S. CONTEXT; PROCEEDINGS.** *Canada-United States Law Journal*, Vol. 15, 1989, 331 pp.

Partial contents.—The importance of innovation to the U.S. in the world competitive context, by Paul F. Oreffice.—The context for innovation in Japan, by Kazuo Nomura.

D010. **ENERGY VS. ENVIRONMENT: THE WRITING ON THE WALL.** *Tokyo Business Today*, July 1989, pp. 34–37.

Japan's booming economy and lower energy prices have created large increases in domestic energy consumption. But the increased energy demand will create future energy shortages, leading to further conflict between nuclear power proponents and opponents.

D011. Ferguson, C.H. **AMERICA'S HIGH-TECH DECLINE.** *Foreign Policy*, No. 74, Spring 1989, pp. 123–144.

Argues that advanced information technology is profoundly changing global competition, both commercial and military....As this transformation progresses, the United States is being gradually but pervasively eclipsed by Japan....More significant, the long-term structural patterns of U.S.–Japanese interaction in finance and high technology imply a future of U.S. decline and dependence on Japan. Moreover, the behavior of the embryonic though rapidly advancing Japanese defense industry suggests that this prediction holds for military technology as well as for commercial activities. Concludes that strategic bargaining with Japan must therefore become a consideration of the first order in U.S. policy.

D012. Ferguson, C.H. **COMPUTERS AND THE COMING OF THE U.S. KEIRETSU.** *Harvard Business Review*, Vol. 68, July–Aug. 1990, pp. 55–70.

Contends that U.S. and European information technology companies face a stark choice: cooperate or become vassals of their Japanese competitors—hang together or hang separately. Claims that the "the endangered list" includes most of the U.S. and European computer, office equipment, and imaging industries such as Apple, DEC, Xerox, Kodak, Olivetti, Philips, and Siemens. Includes brief histories of Japan's keiretsu and Japan's computer industry by Marie Anchordoguy.

D013. **FORUM: JAPAN–U.S. RELATIONS.** *Congressional Research Service Review*, Vol. 10, July 1989, pp. 1–23.

Contents—A more open Japanese market?, by R.A. Ahearn. Japan–U.S. trade: looking ahead, by W.H. Cooper. Technology policy in Japan and the Unites States, by G.J. McLoughlin. Japanese investment in the United States, by J.K. Jackson. Japan's emergence as a leading foreign aid donor, by L.K. Nowels. Japan's expanding economic role and influence in Asia, by R.P. Cronin. Burden sharing and power sharing, by L.A. Niksch. Japan and an East Asian trading bloc, by D.K. Nanto.

D014. Gray, J.E. and Nakayama, Y. (Eds.). **U.S.-JAPAN ENERGY POLICY CONSIDERATIONS FOR THE 1990.** New York: University Press of America, 1988, 104 pp.

D015. Hansen, K. **MAKING NUCLEAR POWER WORK: LESSONS FROM AROUND THE WORLD.** *Technology Review*, Vol. 92, Feb.–Mar. 1989, pp. 30–38,40.

Presents the results of an MIT study of nuclear operations from 1975–1984 in Japan, Sweden, France, Switzerland, West Germany, and the U.S. Findings suggest that the key to improving the U.S. nuclear industry lies not in changing the system within which utilities operate, but rather in implementing managerial reforms that have proven crucial to success elsewhere.

D016. Hayashi, T. **THE JAPANESE EXPERIENCE IN TECHNOLOGY: FROM TRANSFER TO SELF-RELIANCE.** New York: United Nations Press, ISBN 92-808-0566-5, 294 pp.

Japan's rapid transformation from an agrarian society to a highly industrialized modern nation has been the object of much debate and interest. This book examines technology and development in Japan beginning in the Meiji period (1868–1912), through the critical post-war years and up to the uncertainty and new challenges of the 1980s as well as the birth of the Japanese-style manager to the role of the general trading company. An interesting and valuable book for anyone who wants to better understand the roots of Japanese technological success, or for those who want to apply the lessons learned by Japan.

D017. Heaton, G.R., Jr. **COOPERATIVE R&D....IN JAPAN.** *Chemtech*, Vol. 20, Jan. 1990, pp. 14–17.

The Japanese experience shows that a successful cooperative research system requires a delicate balance between government support and industry leadership—a balance that the United States has yet to achieve.

D018. **HIGH-TEMPERATURE SUPERCONDUCTIVITY IN PERSPECTIVE.** Washington: Office of Technology Assessment, G.P.O., 1990, 127 pp.

Focuses on the technology itself and the spectrum of potential applications. Presents an OTA survey comparing industry investment in superconductivity research and development in Japan and the U.S.

D019. Hobday, M. **SEMICONDUCTORS: CREATIVE DESTRUCTION OR U.S. INDUSTRIAL DECLINE?** *Futures*, Vol. 22, July–Aug. 1990, pp. 571–585.

In the context of fears of U.S. industrial decline, particularly vis-a-vis Japan, important new developments in the semiconductor industry are examined. Design innovations and advanced manufacturing technology are key factors influencing competitiveness in this industry, and the notion of decoupling is posited to explain the industrial restructuring that is occurring. After reviewing U.S. policies in this regard, the question of U.S. decline vs. future U.S. prosperity and dynamism in this sector is addressed.

D020. **IMPACTS OF ROBOTICS ON MANUFACTURING: SPECIAL ISSUE.** *Technological Forecasting and Social Change*, Vol. 35, Apr. 1989, whole issue p. 297.

Partial contents—Robotization in Japanese manufacturing industries, by H. Ishitani and Y. Kaya. International comparisons of industrial robot penetration, by A. Tani. The impact of electronics and information on the future trends and applications of CIM technologies, by J. Ranta. Flexible manufacturing systems (FIMS): current diffusion and main advantages, by I. Tchiojv and R. Sheinin.

D021. **INTERNATIONAL TRENDS IN CANCER MORTALITY IN FRANCE, WEST GERMANY, ITALY, JAPAN, ENGLAND AND WALES, AND THE U.S.A.** *Lancet*, Vol. 336, Aug. 25, 1990, pp. 474–481.

Age-specific worldwide trends in cancer mortality were reviewed, with emphasis on cancer sites where increases have been reported in the U.S.A. Cancer rates vary by factors as high as 30 between all countries, and 5-fold within and between industrialized countries. In Italy, Japan, Federal Republic of Germany, England and Wales, and the U.S.A., patterns of cancer mortality have shifted uniformly over the past two decades.

D022. **JAPAN FORGING AGGRESSIVE SPACE DEVELOPMENT PACE.** *Aviation Week and Space Technology*, Vol. 133, Aug. 13, 1990, pp. 36–42,62–67,70–72.

Contents—Japanese accelerate space program for 21st century. Japan's new H-2 launch site rivals largest U.S., European facilities. Mitsubishi leads privatization effort as first H-2 boosters are fabricated. Space agency considers doubling size of HOPE unmanned space vehicle. Japanese earth satellites spawn multiple user groups.

D023. Kalayama, R. **WILL IT FLY?** *Business Tokyo*, Vol. 4, Feb. 1990, pp. 18–20,22–24.

Briefly describes the fortune of the Japanese aircraft industry since the Second World War. Down plays the danger to the U.S. aircraft industry's technological superiority of cooperation agreements with Japanese companies. Looks at the Japanese aircraft industry's future.

D024. Katayama, R. and Colarresso, D. **SUPERTRAIN!** *Business Tokyo*, Vol. 4, Oct. 1990, pp. 20,22–25.

Describes the work of two competing Japanese companies who are developing high speed magnetic levitation trains. Looks at what the U.S. should be doing in maglev R&D.

D025. Kato, K. **JAPAN AND THE ENVIRONMENT.** *Environment*, Vol. 31, July–Aug. 1989, pp. 4–5.

In a letter to the editor, the director of Japan's Office of Planning and Research in the Environment Agency responds to criticism of the 1988 White Paper on the Environment in Japan.

D026. Kingery, J.C. **THE U.S.–JAPAN SEMICONDUCTOR ARRANGEMENT AND THE GATT: OPERATING IN A LEGAL VACUUM.** *Stanford Journal of International Law*, Vol. 25, spring 1989, pp. 467–497.

Article looks at the U.S.–Japan Semiconductor Arrangement and at objects raised by other nations that such an agreement is inconsistent with GATT rules and may actually create a cartel.

D027. Komatsu, N. **JAPAN'S STEEL INDUSTRY IS RESTRUCTURING ITS WAY BACK TO PROFITABILITY.** *Tokyo Business Today*, Vol. 57, Nov. 1989, pp. 40–46.

Describes the dramatic turnaround of the Japanese steel industry since 1986. The industry's restructuring can be divided into three broad areas: cost cuts achieved through major production rationalization, overseas business expansion, and the transfer of surplus personnel, capital, assets and other management resources into high-growth business sectors.

D028. Kubota, H. **STATE OF THE ART OF COMPOSITING IN JAPAN.** *BioCycle*, Vol. 30, Aug. 1989, pp. 67–69.

Presents information given at a symposium in Trento, Italy in June 1989 which provides important data on how composting relates to Japanese waste management methods.

D029. Lepkowski, W. **JAPAN'S SCIENCE AND TECHNOLOGY AIM TOWARD GLOBALIZATION.** *Chemical and Engineering News*, Vol. 67, May 8, 1989, pp. 7–14.

Japan's technical culture—a kind of big, consensual group-think—is distinct from that of the West. Japan brings a new set of values to science and technology, which it sees as one system, with technology, not science, as the intellectual driving force. And it always looks ahead, to the next market, the next phase of research and technology, the next correlation of technological and industrial forces.

D030. Lewis, G. **COMPUTERS: JAPAN COMES ON STRONG.** *Business Week*, No. 3130, Oct. 23, 1989, pp. 104–107,110,112.

Predicts that Japanese computer makers will soon make gains against America's dominance in the microcomputer industry.

D031. Marshall, P.G. **PHOTONICS: NEXT U.S. HIGH-TECH SURRENDER.** Washington: *Congressional Quarterly*, 1990, pp 19–31.

Warns that photonics—the use of photons (light) to gather, store, transmit or manipulate information—may be the next emerging technology that the U.S. could lose its lead to Japan.

D032. Masatomi, F. **HIGH TECHNOLOGY IN THE HIMALAYAS.** *Japan Quarterly*, Vol. 36, July–Sept. 1989, pp. 282–286.

Describes the implementation of the Rural Telecommunication Network Improvement Project in Nepal with Japanese economic assistance and in cooperation with the Japanese Ministry of Posts and Telecommunications. Argues that the project is an example of valid use of high-technology in a developing country.

D033. Mayama, T. **THE JAPAN MARINE SCIENCE AND TECHNOLOGY CENTER.** *Oceanus*, Vol. 30, spring 1989, pp. 27–47.

Seven articles describe the functions and work of the Japan Marine Science and Technology Center (JAMSTEC).

D034. Miller, A.S. **THREE REPORTS ON JAPAN AND THE GLOBAL ENVIRONMENT.** *Environment*, Vol. 31, July–Aug. 1989, pp. 25–29.

Reviews three Japanese reports on Japan and global environmental issues. Reviewed are: White Paper on the Environment in Japan 1988: Japan's Contribution Toward the Conservation of the Global Environment; Japan's Activities to Cope with Global Environmental Problems: Japan's Contribution Toward a Better Global Environment; and, Interim Report on Global Warming.

D035. Nagasaki, F. **THE CASE FOR SCIENTIFIC WHALING.** *Nature*, Vol. 344, Mar. 15, 1990, pp. 189–190.

Commercial whaling by Japan, the Soviet Union and Iceland has been widely condemned. But until scientific studies of whale populations are carried out, an informed decision about commercial whaling cannot be made.

D036. Narin, F. and Frame, J.D. **THE GROWTH OF JAPANESE SCIENCE AND TECHNOLOGY.** *Science*, Vol. 245, Aug. 1989, pp. 600–605.

Focuses on five quantitative indicators of technological and scientific capacity: the number of U.S. patents held by Japanese inventors (a measure of Japanese technological size); the extent to which these patents are cited by other patents (a measure of Japanese technological impact); the extent to which these patents cite the non-patent literature (a measure of the linkage of Japanese technology to science); the number of Japanese papers published in the world's mainstream scientific literature (a measure of Japanese scientific size); and the extent to which these papers are cited in the literature (a measure of Japanese scientific impact).

D037. **1990 UPDATE ON JAPANESE RESEARCH AND DEVELOPMENT.** Washington: Japan Economic Institute, 1990, 23 pp.

Because of Japan's new economic might foreigners want Japan to go beyond simple equality in the research field and are urging it to assume the role of teacher in some areas. Many Japanese agree that sharing technology is one way their country can play a positive leading role in the international community. Others view technology-sharing as a way to pay the debt Japan owes foreigners who openly shared their scientific and technological resources when, as a war-ravaged nation, it sought to rebuild.

D038. Patterson, W. **COAL COMES BACK AS A GAS.** *New Scientist*, Vol. 122, Apr. 29, 1989, pp. 50–53.

Reports on technologies for coal gasification including commercial designs attracting Western Europe, the U.S. and Japan.

D039. Reina, P. and Usui, N. **SUNKEN TUBE TUNNELS PROLIFERATE: CONSTRUCTION TECHNIQUES DIFFER AMONG CONTINENTS, BUT MORE TUBES ARE BEING BUILT.** ENR (*Engineer News-Record*), Vol. 223, July 13, 1989, pp. 30–33,37.

D040. Saito, S. **JAPAN'S SPACE POLICY.** *Space Policy*, Vol. 5, Aug. 1989, pp. 193–200.

Describes the formation of the Space Activities Commission as (Japan's) primary policy-making body, and of the National Space Development Agency, which oversees the development of space technology. The fundamental guidelines governing space activities are explained, and a detailed breakdown is given of projects agreed for the coming years.

D041. Sakita, M. **RESTRUCTURING OF THE JAPANESE NATIONAL RAILWAYS: REVIEW AND ANALYSIS.** *Transportation Quarterly*, Vol. 43, Jan. 1989, pp. 29–45.

Discusses the restructuring of the Japanese National Railways (JNR) which was broken up in 1987 into twelve private corporations, collectively called the Japan Railway (JR) Group.

D042. **SCIENCE, TECHNOLOGY, AND THE U.S. ECONOMY.** Economic Report of the President, transmitted to Congress January 1989. Washington, G.P.O., 1989, p. 223–253.

Provides "an economic perspective on the debate over the appropriate policies to ensure the continued contribution of science and technology to U.S. economic growth, and examines changes in institutions and incentives over the longer term."

D043. Shatz, M. **JAPAN'S TANGLED DRIFT NETS.** *Tokyo Business Today*, Vol. 57, Dec. 1989, pp. 50–51.

The debate over drift net fishing is heating up with calls for an international ban. As with other issues involving the environment sovereignty and livelihood, there are no easy answers.

D044. Slaughter, S. and Utterback, J. **U.S. RESEARCH AND DEVELOPMENT: AN INTERNATIONAL COMPARATIVE ANALYSIS.** *Business in the Contemporary World*, Vol. 2, winter 1990, pp. 27–35.

Examines the research and development funding and manpower capacities of the United States compared to Japan, West Germany, France, and the United Kingdom. Emphasizes that skilled human resources are necessary to create and design new products.

D045. **SPECIAL ISSUE ON EVALUATION OF GOVERNMENT INNOVATION PROGRAMS.** *Research Policy*, Vol. 18, Dec. 1989, whole issue, pp. 309–393.

Contents—Evaluation of government innovation programs: introduction, by J.D. Roessner. Evaluations of innovation programs in selected European countries, by F. Meyer-Krahmer and P.Montigny. Nordic experiences of the evaluation of technical research and development, by E. Ormala. Evaluating government innovation programs: Lessons from the U.S. experience, by J.D. Roessner. Japanese-style evaluation systems for R and D projects: the MIT experience, by M. Tanaka. Evaluation of programs promoting technological innovation the Australian experience, by R. McKeon and J.A. Ryan.

D046. Spero, D.M. **PATENT PROTECTION OR PIRACY—A CEO VIEWS JAPAN.** *Harvard Business Review*, Vol. 68, Sept.–Oct. 1990, pp. 58–60,62,64–67.

A CEO of a fast growing advanced technology company describes the experiences of his company, Fusion Systems, in dealing with Japan's patent system, its hazards, the true costs of mistakes, and some guideposts for maneuvering through this perilous environment.

D047. **STAYING AHEAD BY FOLLOWING.** *Asian Business*, Vol. 26, Apr. 1990, pp. 24–26,28–30,32–33.

Toyota is no trailblazer. But then, it doesn't need to be. Profiles the Japanese giant auto maker and examines its policies and its plans.

D048. **SUPERCOMPUTER BOUT.** *Business Tokyo*, Vol. 4, Apr. 1990, pp. 30–35.

Describes the struggle Cray Research, Inc., an American producer of supercomputers, faces in selling its product in Japan.

D049. Tanzer, A. and Simon, R. **WHY JAPAN LOVES ROBOTS AND WE DON'T.** *Forbes*, Vol. 145, Apr. 16, 1990, pp. 148,150–153.

Always looking to the future, Japanese businesses are pinning many of their industrial hopes on increasing use of factory robots. So what if robots don't pay back their investment right away? They are a great bet for improving manufacturing quality and countering rising labor costs.

D050. Tatsuno, S.M. **JAPAN'S MOVE TOWARD CREATIVITY.** *GAO Journal*, No. 9, summer 1990, pp. 13–18.

Having mastered quality assurance, the Japanese are now eyeing America's last bastions of expertise—basic research and breakthrough thinking.

D051. Taylor, A., III. **HERE COME JAPAN'S NEW LUXURY CARS.** *Fortune*, Vol. 120, Aug. 14, 1989, pp. 62–66.

First out of the gate, Toyota's Lexus is as good as, or better than, more expensive German makes. But will American buyers forgo Teutonic mystique?

D052. Taylor, A., III. **WHY TOYOTA KEEPS GETTING BETTER AND BETTER AND BETTER.** *Fortune*, Vol. 122, Nov. 19, 1990, pp. 66–72,74,76,79.

Success never gets in the way of constant improvement. Here's how the world's best auto maker works harder than ever to avoid 'large-corporation disease.'

D053. **TECHNOLOGICAL INNOVATION AND INDUSTRIAL POLICY: CHOICE AND DIRECTION FOR JAPAN.** *Japanese Viewpoint*, Vol. 2, Autumn 1989, whole issue, p. 41.

Contents—Management strategy for R and D and industrial policy, by Y. Ito. Prospects for management strategy and technological innovation in the Japanese chemical industry, by N. Yoda. TBR symposium: panel discussion on Japan's industrial technology policy and globalization for the twenty-first century, by N. Yoda. Management policy and strategy for R and D, by T. Nakahara. Prospects for carbon fiber reinforced composites, by H. Aotani. Challenge-and-response and corporate culture, by F. Taniguchi.

D054. Teresko, J. **JAPAN'S NEW IDEA.** *Industry Week,* Vol. 239, Sept. 3, 1990, pp. 39,42–44,46,48,52,56,58,62,65,68–69.

After decades of getting their production floors in order, the Japanese are focusing now on technology to change the way they compete. Where price and quality were once their primary competitive tools, Japanese manufacturers are adding technological innovation—in both the product and the manufacturing process itself. Where they once sacrificed short-term profits just to dominate a market, the Japanese are extending that philosophy to boost both R and D and process development.

D055. Teresko, J. **MANUFACTURING IN JAPAN: BEYOND THE STEREOTYPE.** *Industry Week,* Vol. 201, Sept. 4, 1989, pp. 35–36,38,42,46,50,59–60,62,64,66,68,70.

Contends that in contrast to American manufacturing practices, the Japanese slowly and methodically have amassed effective, simple, and usually low-cost improvements. Claims that although the Japanese approach to production and quality management has its roots deep in the country's unique culture, the systems can travel well to Western settings because their successful implementation depends upon people and management.

D056. Toshihiko, I. **MISPLACED PRIORITIES IN WASTE DISPOSAL.** *Japan Echo,* Vol. 16, winter 1990, pp. 73–77.

Interviews Ide Toshihiko, former mayor of Numazu, Japan, and developer of the "Numazu method" of rubbish collection. Regarded as a model in Japan, the method requires residents to sort their waste into burnable, unburnable, and recyclable fractions, which are collected and processed separately. Ide discusses the complex problems of waste disposal and proposes radical reform.

D057. Toshio, W. **A FLAWED APPROACH TO FOREIGN LABOR.** *Japan Echo,* Vol. 17, Spring 1990, pp. 45–50.

Claims that Japan must break the vicious circle in which a thriving underground labor market attracts swelling numbers of foreigners, who further invigorate the market. To eradicate the market, laborers entering Japan must be given legal recognition and granted equal status with Japan's own workers. Proposes an employment-permit system to accommodate foreign workers.

D058. Treece, J.B. **SHAKING UP DETROIT: HOW JAPANESE CAR MAKERS ARE BEATING THE BIG THREE ON THEIR OWN TURF.** *Business Week,* No. 3119, Aug. 14, 1989, pp. 74–80.

Concludes that change is unavoidable for both labor and management. U.S. auto makers must apply the lessons they learn from the transplants. If they don't, their place will be taken by another U.S. car maker—with a Japanese name.

D059. Tully, S. **NOW JAPAN'S AUTOS PUSH INTO EUROPE.** *Fortune*, Vol. 121, Jan. 29, 1990, pp. 96–98, pp. 102,106.

The world's biggest market will boom in the 1990s, and the Japanese—long stifled by quotas—are moving to attack. Looks at the move by Japanese producers to establish production facilities in Western Europe and at the efforts of long-time American and European producers to compete.

D060. **U.S. CONGRESS. HOUSE. COMMITTEE ON ENERGY AND COMMERCE. SUBCOMMITTEE ON TELECOMMUNICATIONS AND FINANCE.**

Public policy implications of advanced television systems; a staff report. Washington, D.P.O., 1989, p. 809. At head of title: 101st Congress, 1st session, committee spring, 101-E.

D061. **U.S. CONGRESS. HOUSE. COMMITTEE ON SCIENCE, SPACE, AND TECHNOLOGY. SUBCOMMITTEE ON SCIENCE, RESEARCH AND TECHNOLOGY.**

The Federal research policy for semiconductors. Hearing, 101st Congress, 2nd session. Mar. 29, 1990, Washington, G.P.O., 1990, p. 113. Serial no. 114.

D062. **U.S. CONGRESS. HOUSE. COMMITTEE ON SCIENCE, SPACE, AND TECHNOLOGY. SUBCOMMITTEE ON SCIENCE, RESEARCH AND TECHNOLOGY.**

U.S./Japan Science and Technology Agreement. Hearing, 100th Congress, 2nd session, July 13, 1988. Washington, G.P.O., 1989, p. 99. Serial no. 148.

D063. **U.S. CONGRESS. HOUSE. COMMITTEE ON SMALL BUSINESS. SUBCOMMITTEE ON REGULATION, BUSINESS OPPORTUNITIES, AND ENERGY.**

U.S. wood products competitiveness: timber, taxes, and trade. Joint hearing before the Subcommittee on Regulation, Business Opportunities, and Energy of the Committee on Small Business, House of Representatives, and the Subcommittee on Conservation and Forestry of the Committee on Agriculture, Nutrition, and Forestry, United States Senate, 101st Congress, 1st session, Washington, G.P.O., 1989, p. 288. Serial no. 101–15. Hearing held in Portland, OR, July 8, 1989.

D064. **U.S. CONGRESS. HOUSE. COMMITTEE ON WAYS AND MEANS.**

Enforcement of the United States–Japan semiconductor agreement; report to accompany H. Res. 146. (Washington, G.P.O.), 1989, p. 3. (Report, House, 101st Congress, 1st session, no. 101–66).

D065. **U.S. CONGRESS. HOUSE. SENATE. COMMITTEE ON COMMERCE, SCIENCE, AND TRANSPORTATION.**

Competitiveness challenge facing the U.S. industry. Hearing, 101st Congress, 2nd session. May 11–23, 1990, Washington, G.P.O., 1990, p. 143. (Hearing, Senate, 101st Congress, 2nd session, S. Hrg. 101–798). Hears testimony about the economic strategy being pursued by Japan, particularly the aspect of picking winners or targeting key technologies for government support.

D066. **U.S. CONGRESS. HOUSE. SENATE. COMMITTEE ON COMMERCE, SCIENCE, AND TRANSPORTATION. SUBCOMMITTEE ON FOREIGN COMMERCE AND TOURISM.**

Japanese patent policy. Hearing, 101st Congress, 1st session. Feb. 28, 1989, Washington, G.P.O., 1989, p. 94. (Hearing, Senate, 101st Congress, 1st session, S. Hrg. 101–19).

D067. **U.S. CONGRESS. SENATE, COMMITTEE ON COMMERCE, SCIENCE, AND TRANSPORTATION. SUBCOMMITTEE ON FOREIGN COMMERCE AND TOURISM.**

Japanese space industry—an American challenge. Hearing, 101st Congress, 1st session. Oct. 4, 1989, Washington, G.P.O., 1989, p. 55. (Hearing, Senate, 101st Congress, 1st session, S. Hrg. 101–346).

D068. **U.S. CONGRESS. SENATE. COMMITTEE ON FINANCE. SUBCOMMITTEE ON INTERNATIONAL TRADE.**

Super 301: effectiveness in opening foreign markets. Hearing, 101st Congress, 2nd session. Apr. 27, 1990, Washington, G.P.O., 1990, p. 141. (Hearing, 101st Congress, 2nd session, S. Hrg. 101–995). Includes reprint of a report by Cray Research, Inc. (The Japanese public sector: problems and prospects for U.S. supercomputer vendors).

D069. **U.S. CONGRESS. SENATE. COMMITTEE ON FOREIGN RELATIONS.**

International environmental agenda for the 101st Congress. Hearing, 101st Congress, 1st session, Apr. 20, 1989, Washington, G.P.O., 1989, p. 276. (Hearing, Senate, 101st Congress, 1st session, S. Hrg. 101–184).

D070. **U.S. CONGRESS. SENATE. COMMITTEE ON GOVERNMENTAL AFFAIRS.**

Prospects for development of a U.S. HDTV industry. Hearing, 101st Congress, 1st session, Aug. 1, 1989, Washington, G.P.O., 1989, p. 577. (Hearing, Senate, 101st Congress, 1st session, S. Hrg. 101–226).

D071. Valery, N. **JAPANESE TECHNOLOGY: THINKING AHEAD.** *Economist*, Vol. 313, Dec. 2, 1989, pp. 1,3–9,12–18.

States that the real driving force behind Japan's technological juggernaut is not the nudging or cajoling by government, but the sheer weight of private investment.

D072. **THE WASTE-DISPOSAL PROBLEM.** *Echo*, Vol. 16, winter 1990, pp. 67–72.

In this examination of municipal waste disposal in Japan, the author focuses on the pollution caused by the treatment of refuse, citing examples of ways in which toxic gases, heavy metals, and other substances find their way into the environment. He calls for stepped-up efforts to reduce waste volumes and promote recycling, such as charging people directly for collection services and paying subsidies for the recycling of paper.

D073. Womack, J.P., Jones, D.T. and Roos, D. **HOW LEAN PRODUCTION CAN CHANGE THE WORLD.** *New York Times*, Sept. 23, 1990, pp. 20–23,34,38.

From factory floor to dealer's showroom, Japan's revolutionary way of making and marketing cars is chipping away at the foundations of mass production. Adapted from a forthcoming book (The Machine that Changed the World).

D074. Woodruff, D. **A NEW ERA FOR AUTO QUALITY.** *Business Week,* No. 3184, Oct. 22, 1990, pp. 84–87,90–91,94,96.

Discusses the new Japanese philosophy of things gone right (miryokuteki hinshitsu) which is making cars that are more than reliable, that fascinate, bewitch, and delight.

D075. Yoichi, K. **THREATS TO THE GLOBAL ECOSYSTEM.** *Japan Echo,* Vol. 17, spring 1990, pp. 65–68.

During an interview, the author, a Japanese scientist and member of the United Nations Science and Technology Advisory Committee for Development, expresses his opinions about global warming and ozone depletion.

D076. Yoshikawa, A. **THE OTHER DRUG WAR: U.S.–JAPAN TRADE IN PHARMACEUTICALS.** *California Management Review,* Vol. 31, winter 1989, pp. 76–90.

The pharmaceutical industry is one of the few high-technology areas in which the United States still maintains a favorable balance of trade with Japan. Today, the Japanese pharmaceutical market is experiencing a major structural reorganization as a result of both scientific breakthroughs in the development of biotechnology and government measures to liberalize trade under pressure abroad. This reorganization process will provide many new opportunities for American and other foreign firms, but it will also bring them new challenges from increasingly competitive and internationally oriented Japanese drug companies.

E. EDUCATION; CULTURE; EMPLOYMENT; LAW; PUBLIC OPINION

E001. Abe, M.A. **UNDERCURRENTS OF FRUSTRATION AND ROLES OF GAIATSU IN JAPAN: EMERGING DIVISION IN ECONOMIC STRATA AND THE UNIFICATION OF LABOR MOVEMENT.** *Asian Profile*, Vol. 17, Oct. 1989, pp 397–406.

Argues that while Japan has become one of the most affluent nations in the world, some of its basic living standards lad far behind those in advanced western nations. Points out that pressures from abroad (gaiatsu) will force Japanese leaders to face reality and heed the needs of the people rather than the vested interests. Only then the standard of living in Japan will start improving.

E002. Akhavan-Majid, R. **TELECOMMUNICATIONS POLICYMAKING IN JAPAN: THE 1980s AND BEYOND.** *Telecommunications Policy*, Vol. 14, Apr 1990, pp 159–168.

The major law which provided for privatization of Nippon Telegraph and Telephone (NTT) in 1984 is up for review by the Japanese government in April 1990. Given the continuing domination of Japan's telecommunications market by NTT, ultimate divestiture of the privatized NTT remains a likely outcome of the review.

E003. Allen, G.C. **MODERN JAPAN AND ITS PROBLEMS.** The Athlone Press, 1990, 226 pp.

One of the chief objects of the author, is to emphasize what he conceives to be the fundamental characteristics of Japan's civilization and to indicate the extent to which they have been modified by Western influences. He tries to show that Japan breathed into the institutions and systems which she imported from Europe a spirit of her own—a spirit which had little in common with that of the countries from which those new institutions and systems were drawn. In consequence, there has arisen, even in those phases of Japan's life which we consider most modern and Western, a mass of novel problems and of phenomena unfamiliar to European eyes. Although some of these problems—social, political and industrial—may bear a superficial resemblance to our own, yet they seldom admit of Western solutions; for they are the problems of a civilization with different aims and values.

E004. Bednarzik, R.W. and Shiells, C.R. **LABOR MARKET CHANGES AND ADJUSTMENTS: HOW DO THE U.S. AND JAPAN COMPARE?** *Monthly Labor Review*, Vol. 112, Feb 1989, pp 31–42.

Both countries are flexible in how they react to structural changes in the labor market, with each using different methods and programs to adjust to such changes rather quickly.

E005. Bobrow, D.B. **JAPAN IN THE WORLD: OPINION FROM DEFEAT TO SUCCESS.** *Journal of Conflict Resolution*, Vol. 33, Dec 1989, pp 571–604.

A survey of Japanese public opinion in the post-occupation period finds that little support appears for strong, ongoing shifts from international passivism to activism, alignment to equidistance, dependence to autonomy, military minimization to effort, or lack of guiding principles....Majority opinion is sceptical about the merits of departures from the status quo buttressed by countervailing minorities that support opposed directions of change.

E006. Brooks, R.A. **A JAPAN THAT CAN SAY "YES."** Washington: Heritage Foundation, 1990, 16 pp.

Urges U.S. officials to continue pressing Japan to improve the standard of living of its own citizens, to open its domestic retail market to foreign goods, and to end its industrial cartels. Claims it is time now for Japan and the Japanese people to assume the responsibilities that their position in the global trading system requires. Claims that only Japan of the major industrialized countries does not play by the broad rules of that system.

E007. Brown, R.C. **THE FACES OF JAPANESE LABOR RELATIONS IN JAPAN AND THE U.S. AND THE EMERGING LEGAL ISSUES UNDER U.S. LABOR LAWS.** Syracuse: *Journal of International Law and Commerce*, Vol. 15, Winter 1989, pp. 231–255.

Article addresses the policy issues raised by the adaptation of the Japanese traditions of labor relations for use in Japanese factories in the United States.

E008. Chambers, G.S. and Cummins, W.K. **IIE RESEARCH REPORT NO. 20.**

Partial contents.—Taking American higher education to Japan and vice versa.—Development of Japanese overseas education.—Negotiating finances and control.—Who controls the use of public resources?—Issues involving U.S. private institutions.—Issues involving governmental partners.

E009. Choy, J. **EDUCATION REFORM IN JAPAN: WILL THE THIRD TIME BE THE CHARM?** Japan Economic Institute report, No. 45A, Nov. 30, 1990, pp. 1–2.

Identifies issues in Japan's current debate over educational reform: systematic issues, such as the examination system, school/career tracking, and central control; content issues, such as creativity, individuality, and internationalization, quality of graduate education, and moral education, and societal obstacles to reform.

E010. Culkin, D.F. **A LOOK AT JAPANESE WORK AND LEISURE** *Park and Recreation*, Vol. 24, Apr. 1989, pp. 33–37,66.

Describes how much free time the Japanese have during various stages of life and describes the pastimes they pursue. Observes that Japanese infants and preschoolers enjoy full-time unstructured childcare by their mothers, but that life becomes quite structured as soon as school is begun. Japanese youth do learn instrumental music, hobbies, and club activities before the high school years. After-work socializing with colleagues is the norm for young Japanese workers.

E011. Drucker, P.F. **JAPAN'S CHOICES: SOMEBODY'S GAINING ON JAPAN.** *Chemtech*, Vol. 19, June 1989, pp. 336–339.

Examines the economic and social choices Japan must make to adapt to and integrate into the changing international economy. Resistance to Japanese exports by the Western industrialized countries and competition from the newly industrialized countries are forcing Japan to face changes.

E012. Durlabhji, S. **THE INFLUENCE OF CONFUCIANISM AND ZEN ON THE JAPANESE ORGANIZATION.** *Akron Business and Economic Review*, Vol. 21, summer 1990, pp. 31–45.

Suggests that the success of the Japanese work organization as a social system is attributable primarily to Eastern culture: to Confucianism's single-minded search for wa (harmony) and to Zen's more complex vision of human beings. Concepts of Eastern culture have remained somewhat inaccessible to the West; hence, the discussion in this paper is placed in the context of concepts developed in the West.

E013. Eisenach, J. and Cowin, A. **FIGHTING DRUGS IN FOUR COUNTRIES: LESSONS FOR AMERICA?** Washington: Heritage Foundation, 1990, 16 pp.

Assesses the drug policies of Britain, the Netherlands, Japan, and Singapore, concluding that Britain and the Netherlands offer no evidence that drug legalization will help solve the U.S. drug problem. The more strict policies of Japan and Singapore have shown results and may offer some guideposts for American reforms.

E014. **EMERGING ECONOMIC INEQUITIES** *Japan Echo*, Vol. 16, summer 1989, pp. 45–57.

Concedes that the leveling of Japanese society has reversed direction, and the growing disparities in wealth are bringing a new, more sharply differentiated class structure into being. Discusses the influence of political lobbies in the efforts to reduce red tape and reform the tax structure. Superpower Japan, the closet pauper, by T. Nobuaki. Shoddy taxes, shady politics, by I. Mitsuharu.

E015. Fallows, J. **THE HARD LIFE.** *Atlantic Monthly*, Vol. 263, Mar. 1989, pp. 16,18–20,22,24–26.

Maintains that despite crowded living conditions, long working hours, and fewer material rewards than in other industrialized countries, the average Japanese is relatively content with his life style. Contends that the current system in Japan benefits all the moneyed interests (except consumers) and claims that even Japanese consumers would freely choose an anti-consumer system that shields them from frequent layoffs, business turmoil, and other cyclical disruptions. This orientation virtually guarantees continued trade imbalances with the U.S.

E016. Fallows, J. **MORE LIKE US: MAKING AMERICA GREAT AGAIN.** Boston: Houghton Mifflin, 1989, 245 pp.

A personal observation of life in Japan and other Asian nations, countries which are economically robust but culturally and socially closed. Claims that the U.S. can reclaim its political and economic drive by relying on its unique qualities. That means reinventing the American tradition of social mobility, reopening the frontiers that enabled generation of immigrants and their children to start new lives, move up and out, and if necessary start all over again. It means stopping America's drift toward a rigid, class-bound system that sets people apart on the basis of family background and education.

E017. George, B.C., Stanberry, K. and Boss, M. **NEW STEPS TO PROHIBIT INSIDER TRADING IN JAPAN: A SERIOUS COMMITMENT OR SIMPLY SAVING FACE?** *Asian Thought and Society*, Vol. 15, May 1990, pp. 227–235.

Examines the social and economic attitudes in Japan which make insider trading regulations difficult to enforce, explores the historical background of the securities law, discusses the new law and recently-promulgated regulations prohibiting insider trading, and reviews the extraterritorial enforcement agreement regarding international cooperation.

E018. Gleason, A.H. **THE LEVEL OF LIVING IN JAPAN AND THE UNITED STATES: A LONG-TERM INTERNATIONAL COMPARISON.** *Economic Development and Cultural Change*, Vol. 37, Jan. 1989, pp. 261–284.

It is the purpose of this article to evaluate Japan's progress during the past century in raising the level of living of its people and to do this mainly through a comparison with the United States, whose level has often served as a standard for international comparisons.

E019. Halberstam, D. **REFLECTIONS ON JAPAN INC.** *Business Month*, Vol. 133, Feb. 1989, pp. 45–49.

Reflects briefly on those unique characteristics of Japan's corporate culture, educational system, bureaucracy, and value system that have contributed to the economic miracle.

E020. Haruo, S. **ASSET INFLATION AND THE STRAINED SOCIAL FABRIC.** *Japan Echo*, Vol. 17, special issue, 1990, pp. 13–20.

Discusses some of the changes caused by Japan's growing economic success in the nation's social fabric. Calls for a new set of ideals and political goals which will help Japan open up its markets and share its technology with the rest of the world.

E021. Holstein, W.J. **THE JAPANESE POWER GAME: WHAT IT MEANS FOR AMERICA.** New York: Charles Scribner's Sons, 1990, 339 pp.

In a series of revelations, Holstein shows how hopes for political and social change in Japan in the wake of the Recruit scandal were dramatically overblown. It was the challengers to the status quo, not the establishment, who were punished. Nor have the Japanese lost their competitive clout. Even as the Japanese power game is played at home, the Japanese are extending their systems and values to the United States and increasing their influence on American perceptions and politics.

E022. Inoue, K. **MACARTHUR'S JAPANESE CONSTITUTION: A LINGUISTIC AND CULTURAL STUDY OF ITS MAKING.** Chicago: University of Chicago Press, 1991, 378 pp.

In February 1948 General Douglas MacArthur presented the Japanese government with a new constitution for its country, written by his headquarters in ten days. Difficulties in the translation of the document by the Japanese brought out all the differences between the two countries on such basic questions as the relationship between the state and the people, religious freedom, the status of the emperor and the equality of the sexes in marriage. According to the author, the cultural and linguistic barriers were never overcome. Today the American text conforms with our political and cultural traditions, while the Japanese translation is congenial to that nation's values. Indeed, there is a little agreement on the fundamental meaning of key clauses of the constitution. This is a fascinating book for serious students of Japan and cross-cultural problems.

E023. Ito, T. and Kang, K. **BONUSES, OVERTIME, AND EMPLOYMENT: KOREA VS. JAPAN**. Cambridge: National Bureau of Economic Research, 1989, 38 pp.

Concludes that both bonuses and wages in Korea respond to economic conditions much more than their counterparts in Japan. This finding may reflect the fact that the Korean labor market is much closer to a spot market rather than a long-term contract (lifetime employment) market. Hence the bonus/wage ratio is apparently insensitive to economic conditions in Korea, unlike Japan.

E024. Itoh, H. **JAPANESE SUPREME COURT: CONSTITUTIONAL POLICIES.** Markus Wiener Pub., Inc., 1989, ISBN 0-910129-91-9, 307 pp.

E025. Katz, L.F. and Revenga, A.L. **CHANGES IN THE STRUCTURE OF WAGES: THE U.S. VERSUS JAPAN**. Cambridge: National Bureau of Economic Research, 1989, 34 pp.

Presents an overview of changes in educational wage differentials in Japan and the U.S. and discusses movements in the pattern of earnings in each country. Considers the role of demographic factors, marcoeconomic conditions, structural demand shifts, and deunionization in explaining movements in the structure of wages.

E026. Kelman, S. **THE "JAPANIZATION" OF AMERICA?** *Public Interest*, No. 98, winter 1990, pp. 70–83.

Examines the cultural impact of Japanese investment in the U.S. Concludes that the debate over cultural is crucial to the debate over America's internationalization; if that debate is to be resolved constructively, we must think explicitly about how to conduct it.

E027. Levin, P.J. and Wolfson, J. **HEALTH CARE IN THE BALANCE: JAPANESE EURYTHMY.** *Hospital and Health Services Administration*, Vol. 34, fall 1989, pp. 311–232.

Japan's health care delivery system fits neatly into the island nation's well-ordered, carefully balanced infrastructure. The organization and operation of Japan's health system reflects the quest for harmony and balance, or eurythmy, of Japanese culture. While Japan's economic success has attracted considerable attention among management scientists, the health care system that fuels and nurtures the health status of its hyperproductive workforce has not been a topic of much interest. The organization and management of Japan's health services delivery system are analyzed in this article.

E028. **LIFESTYLES IN AN AFFLUENT SOCIETY.** *Japan Echo*, Vol. 16, summer 1989, pp. 28–44.

Contents—Learning to live the good life, by Fujioka Wakao. College life today: the economics of indulgence, by S. Masumi. Woman and man in modern Japan, by T. Masatoshi.

E029. Lincoln, J.R. **EMPLOYEE WORK ATTITUDES AND MANAGEMENT PRACTICE IN THE U.S. AND JAPAN: EVIDENCE FROM A LARGE COMPARATIVE SURVEY.** *California Management Review*, Vol. 32, fall 1989, pp. 89–106.

Surveys 106 Japanese and U.S. factories and 8,302 of their employees on how work attitudes and motivation differ between Japanese and U.S. employees and whether management practice and organizational design can account for those differences. The article concludes that practices such as quality circles, the ringi system, centralized authority combined with de facto participation, employee services, seniority compensation, and enterprise unions do, in fact, help to explain the 'commitment gap' that divides the Japanese from the U.S. manufacturing workforce. When these and similar practices appear in U.S. factories, similar positive changes in employee work attitudes result.

E030. Martin, L.G. **THE GRAYING OF JAPAN.** *Population Bulletin*, Vol. 44, July 1989, whole issue, p. 42.

With the highest life expectancy on earth, the Japanese potentially face long periods of retirement, as well as the possibility of long periods of disability. Family relations, demography, social expenditures, labor trends, and Japan's future are discussed.

E031. Martin, L.G. **JAPAN COPES WITH ITS "HONORABLE ELDERS": RETIREMENT AND HEALTH BENEFIT SYSTEMS IN JAPAN.** EBRI issue brief, No. 92, July 1989, pp. 1–17.

Adapted from the Graying of Japan, by Linda Martin with editorial assistance from Susan Kalish. In Japan, as in the United States, the aging of the population is challenging public and private health and retirement benefit systems and family support systems for the elderly.

E032. **MEDICINE, MORALITY, AND CULTURE: INTERNATIONAL BIOETHICS.** *Hastings Center Report*, Vol. 19, July–Aug. 1989, pp. 1–31.

Contents—From global rationing to target setting in the U.K., by R. Klein. In Ghana, conflict and complimentarily, by J. Hevi. Caring for the elderly and Malta's national health scheme, by E. Agius. Ethical responsibility in the German Democratic Republic, by S. Tannenberger. Health care ethics in Kuwait, by M. Al Mutawa. The new health service in New Zealand, by B. Brookes. In Turkey, new goals for health care, by N.H. Fisek. Ethics and genetics: an international survey, by D.C. Wertz and J.C. Fletcher.

E033. Mieczkowski, S. **THE RISE AND FALL OF THE JAPANESE STUDENT FEDERATION (ZENGAKUREN).** *Asian Thought and Society*, Vol. 14, Jan. 1989, pp. 43–58.

E034. Moffatt, S. **SHOULD YOU WORK FOR THE JAPANESE?** *Fortune*, Vol. 122, Dec. 3, 1990, pp. 107–108,112,116,120.

With a few exceptions, Japanese have been good at managing factory workers. But they really flounder when confronted with hard-driving MBAs, many of whom are women. The egalitarian ethos and emphasis on team effort that go over so well on the shop floor often frustrate managers accustomed to individual responsibility and recognition. And while blue-collar workers enjoy a relatively high level of participation in decision-making, Americans in the front office grouse that real policy-making goes on in Tokyo.

E035. Murdo, P. **CORPORATE BENEFITS AS A COMPETITIVE TOOL IN JAPAN.** Washington: Japan Economic Institute, 1990, 16 pp.

Claims that corporate benefits in Japan are more easily adjusted than standardized pay scales and offer great flexibility in remunerating employees. Says that the current labor shortage has the potential to tilt employee compensation packages toward time-related benefits or other nonwage-related remuneration.

E036. **A NEW SCHOOL OF THOUGHT?** *Far Eastern Economic Review*, Vol. 143, Apr. 6, 1989, pp. 64–66,70,72–73.

A series of four short articles that look at current reforms in the Japanese education system, especially in textbook editing, curriculum, teacher training, and entrance exams, in order to introduce more creative, analytical thinking and less conformist modes in acquiring and using knowledge.

E037. **OVERSEAS CHINESE.** *Free China Review*, Vol. 39, July 1989, whole issue, pp. 4–62.

Partial contents—Humane and beneficial assimilation, by L. Chien-ai. Optimism mixed with tensions, by L. Chien-ai. Investing in a better Malaysia, by L Chien-ai. Aliens in their adopted land, by C. Chang. Survival of the persistent, by T. Yung-li. Making it in Japan, by C. Chang. Hard-earned Aloha, by K. Hung-ting.

E038. Parkinson, L. **JAPAN'S EQUAL EMPLOYMENT OPPORTUNITY LAW: AN ALTERNATIVE APPROACH TO SOCIAL CHANGE.** *Columbia Law Review*, Vol. 89, Apr. 1989, pp. 604–661.

Using almost entirely Japanese language sources, comment examines Japan's Equal Employment Opportunity Law (EEOL), which was passed in 1985 in response both to pressure from abroad and to a changing domestic society. Eschewing legal sanctions to eliminate discrimination in employment, this law instead looks to noncoercive means to achieve social change.

E039. Rapoport, C. **A LOOK INSIDE A JAPANESE SCHOOL.** *Fortune*, Vol. 120, Dec. 4, 1989, pp. 158,160.

Japanese children may be no smarter than those elsewhere, but they undoubtedly work harder. They spend more time in school than do Americans—an average of 220 days a year, vs. 178—and they have more homework. They memorize more too.

E040. Ratcliffe, C.T. **THE INTRICACIES OF JAPANOMICS: STRATEGY FOR INTERNATIONAL COMPETITIVENESS.** *Speaking of Japan*, Vol. 11, June 1990, pp. 12–16.

Argues that Japan has clearly had an industrial strategy, a distinctive Japanomics, characterized by hardheaded pragmatism and minimal attention to economic ideologies. Lists the principal aspects of this strategy. The author is president of International Business Information, K.K., Tokyo.

E041. Rauch, J. **THE TROUBLE WITH JAPAN.** *American Enterprise,* Vol. 1, Mar.–Apr. 1990, pp. 78–82.

Preoccupation with our trade deficit with Japan allows us to gloss over more serious problems: differences in values, commitment to global economic issues, and control of strategic industries.

E042. Richman, L.S. **THE COMING WORLD LABOR SHORTAGE.** *Fortune,* Vol. 121, Apr. 9, 1990, pp. 70–72,74,76–77.

A baby bust will soon shake industrialized economies everywhere. To cope, they must start encouraging immigration and discouraging early retirement. Looks at aging and population trends in Japan, Western Europe, and the U.S.

E043. Ryosuke, O. and Shoichi, S. **JAPANESE CULTURE IN THE MODERN WORLD.** *Japan Echo,* Vol. 16, spring 1989, pp. 69–84.

Series of two articles explore cultural differences between Japan and the West and detail aspects of Japanese culture.

E044. Sassen, S. **THE MOBILITY OF LABOR AND CAPITAL: THE U.S. AND JAPAN.** *Business in the Contemporary World,* Vol. 2, spring 1990, pp. 77–82.

Claims that if the U.S. experience with illegal immigration should take place in Japan, the Japanese may see a growing number of 'tourists' and 'visitors' who are coming into the country, not to visit, but to find gainful employment.

E045. Selby, M. **HUMAN RIGHTS AND UNDOCUMENTED IMMIGRANT WORKERS IN JAPAN.** *Stanford Journal of International Law,* Vol. 26, fall 1989, pp. 325–369.

Japan is certainly not the only country facing the problems of how to deal with foreign immigration and hot to treat its undocumented laborers. In trying to formulate a policy for Japan, the Japanese government and Japanese civic groups have examined the experiences of European countries.

E046. Shoji, K. **JAPAN'S EDUCATION FACTORY.** *Business Tokyo,* Vol. 4, Sept. 1990, pp. 20–25.

Contrasts the educational systems of Japan and the U.S., particularly in discipline, endurance, family support, and quality control. Notes the Japanese emphasis on math education.

E047. **SHOWA: THE JAPAN OF HIROHITO.** *Daedalus,* Vol. 119, summer 1990, whole issue, p. 298.

Partial contents—The idea of Showa, by C. Gluck. The Showa era (1926–1989), by M. Kosaka. The useful war, by J.W. Dower, Japan meets the United States for the second time, by M. Iokibe. The occupation some reflections, by H. Passin. Bringing politics back into Japan, by M. Muramatsu. Money and the Japanese, by S. Royama. The Showa economic experience, by E.J. Lincoln. Regional Japan: the price of prosperity and the benefits of dependency, by W.W. Kelly. The intellectual community of the Showa era, by M. Yamazaki. How they have looked to us, by E. Seidensticker. This issue of Daedalus seeks....to dwell on longer-range historical processes, which help to explain what Japan has become.

E048. Solo, S. **JAPAN DISCOVERS WOMAN POWER.** *Fortune,* Vol. 119, June 19, 1989, pp. 153–154,156–158.

Faced with a labor shortage, Japanese companies are looking to make managers of young college graduates once condemned to be mere 'office ladies.'

E049. Spencer, E.W. **JAPAN AS COMPETITOR.** *Foreign Policy,* No. 78, spring 1990, pp. 153–171.

Claims that success in managing the U.S.–Japanese relationship will come easier if there is recognition that while the two countries share many common values, Americans and Japanese are different and their interests sometimes diverge. Looks at possible scenarios of the Japan–U.S. relationship in the 1990s.

E050. Tai, H. (Ed.) **CONFUCIANISM AND ECONOMIC DEVELOPMENT: AN ORIENTAL ALTERNATIVE.** Washington: Washington Institute for Values in Public Policy, 233 pp.

Partial contents.—The oriental alternative: hypothesis on culture and economy, Hung-chao Tai.—Economic performance in five East Asian countries: a comparative analysis, by Yuan-li Wu and Hung-chao Tai.—Historical factors affecting China's economic underdevelopment, by Hang-sheng Cheng.—Confucianism and Japanese modernization: a study of Shibusawa Eiichi, by Kuo-hui Tai.—The divergent economic development of China and Japan, by Edward F. Hartfield.

E051. Tankha, B. **THE IDEA OF EDUCATION IN MODERN JAPAN.** *China Report,* Vol. 25, Jan.–Mar. 1989, pp. 39–51.

In this paper we shall consider the idea of education during two crucial periods of Japanese history. The first during the Meiji period when the institutions and structures of a modern nation were built, and the second when the United States defeated Japan in World War II and occupied Japan for seven years. These were two periods when, even if we do not see them as breaks, the changes were qualitative in nature and therefore an examination of some of these changes can help us understand how Japanese thinking on education changed.

E052. Thornton, R.Y. and Endo, K. **CONTROLLING CRIME AND DELINQUENCY: A TALE OF TWO CITIES.** *Police Chief,* Vol. 57, Mar. 1990, pp. 54–58.

A cross-cultural comparative study of crime and delinquency prevention methods and techniques in the sister cities of Salem, Oregon, and Kawagoe, Japan. Salem, the capital city of the state of Oregon....Although Salem's population in 1986 was only one-third that of Kawagoe, there were nearly nine times more reported crimes in Salem for that year. The statistics comparing the percentage of crimes cleared by arrest in both cities are even more surprising. In Kawagoe, 69 percent of crimes were cleared by arrest, compared with only 41 percent in Salem.

E053. Tobin, J.J., Wu, D.Y.H and Davidson, D.H. **HOW THREE KEY COUNTRIES SHAPE THEIR CHILDREN.** *World Monitor,* Vol. 2, Apr. 1989, pp. 36–45.

Spending a day with four-year-olds in China, Japan, and the U.S. shows that these cultures have distinctively different aims—and some common goals—as they turn to preschools to preserve values in a time of change.

E054. **THE TROUBLE WITH LAWYERS.** *Business Tokyo*, Vol. 4, Oct. 1990, pp. 26,28–31.

Currently, bengoshi (the highest-ranking of several types of Japanese legal-specialists) are the only professionals authorized to appear in Japanese court and advise on all issues of Japanese law....Because most cross-border transactions involve questions of both U.S. and Japanese law, the partnership/employment ban often makes it necessary for U.S. businesses to retain attorneys from both American and Japanese firms.

E055. van Wolferen, K. **THE ENIGMA OF JAPANESE POWER.** *Fortune*, Vol. 119, May 8, 1989, pp. 150–153.

Excerpt from "The Enigma of Japanese Power," by K. van Wolferen discusses the Japanese political and administrative system. Concludes that in Japan no one is ultimately in charge. Statecraft in Japan has resulted from a balance between semiautonomous groups that share power. This system, minus its military component, consolidated power after the war and is in the process of consolidating it even further. The implications of this are that the Japanese system has no control of itself and can therefore not make the changes desired by Japan's Western allies and trading partners.

E056. van Wolferen, K. **THE ENIGMA OF JAPANESE POWER: PEOPLE AND POLITICS IN A STATELESS NATION.** New York, Alfred A. Knopf, 1989, p. 496.

Examines political, social, economic and administrative power in Japanese society. Argues that it is misleading to go by the familiar institutional labels attached to the evident exercise of power in Japan. The Japanese prime minister is not expected to show much leadership; labor unions organize strikes to be held during lunch breaks; the legislature does not in fact legislate; stockholders never demand dividends; consumer interest groups advocate protectionism; laws are enforced only if they don't conflict too much with the interests of the powerful; and the ruling Liberal Democratic Party is, if anything, conservative and authoritarian, is not really a party and does not in fact rule.

E057. Weisman, S.R. **JAPAN'S IMPERIAL PRESENT.** *New York Times Magazine*, Aug. 26, 1990, pp. 29–30,58,64,74.

Today everyone is fascinated by royalty, one expert says. 'You cannot find one harsh word against the system.'

E058. West, M.D. **THE JAPANESE LEGAL SYSTEM: WHY MANY AMERICANS FAIL.** *Journal of Northeast Asian Studies*, Vol. 8, spring 1989, pp. 20–38.

Argues that the failure of the American trans-Pacific business community to acquaint itself adequately with the unique Japanese legal system has contributed to America's inability to penetrate Japanese markets, the default of many business ventures, and ultimately to the decline of America's economic status relative to Japan.

E059. **WHAT JAPAN THINKS OF US.** *Newsweek*, Vol. 115, Apr. 2, 1990, pp. 18–25.

Examines the results and implications of a phone poll, taken in January 1990, of Japanese opinion of the U.S. and its citizens. Concludes that the message, delivered with increasing un-Japanese candor, is simple: grow up, America. The Japanese believe Americans are overwrought crybabies, grousing about trade problems primarily of their own making—product of a flaccid fiscal policy, an inability to make goods anyone would want to buy. And, many Japanese say, Americans display utter indifference to those facts.

E060. **WOMEN AND THE FAMILY.** *Review of Japanese Culture and Society*, Vol. 3, Dec. 1989, whole issue, p. 10.

Partial contents—Women's labor under patriarchal capitalism in the eighties. Working mothers and families. Family care for the elderly in the United States. Aspects of an aging society. Father-daughter incest. Some thoughts on domestic violence in Japan. Family planning, the state, and the control of fertility. Translation of works written in Japanese, published by Josai University, Tokyo.

E061. Wood, S. **THE JAPANESE MANAGEMENT MODEL: TACIT SKILLS IN SHOP FLOOR PARTICIPATION.** *Work and Occupations*, Vol. 16, Nov. 1989, pp. 446–460.

Suggests that the Japanese workers participation is distinctive insofar as it explicitly involves them in industrial (Kanban) engineering,...(this) derives from the wider innovations....such as just-in-time and the continuous learning program (Kaizen), as well as other aspects of Japanese personnel practice.

E062. **THE WORLD'S (NO.) 1 CUSTOMER.** *Business Tokyo*, Vol. 3, Oct. 1989, pp. 35–29.

Looks at the demographics and economic forces behind Japan's female consumers, who comprise the best-educated generation in Japanese history. By the end of the century Japan's per capita income will be 50% to 100% higher than the U.S. figure, and women will control household spending.

F. AGRICULTURE

F001. Bovard, J. **FARM SUBSIDIES: SEPARATING THE WHEAT FROM THE CHAFF.** *World and I*, Vol. 4, Sept. 1989, pp 106–109.

Analyzes agricultural subsidy policies in three markets: U.S., Europe, and Japan.

F002. **A CHOICES DEBATE ON....JAPANESE BEEF TRADE LIBERALIZATION.** *Choices*, Vol. 4, fourth quarter, 1989, pp. 26–31.

For many years Japan has restricted its beef imports. This set of pro-con articles examines what has happened since Japan agreed to "liberalize" beef imports from other countries, including the U.S. Contents—It may not benefit Americans, by J.M. Alston, C.A. Carter, and L.S. Harvis. It will benefit American agriculture, by W.T. Coyle and J. Dyck.

F003. Hudson, W.J. **THE BASIC MECHANISMS OF JAPANESE FARM POLICY ILLUSTRATED BY: RICE PRICE SUPPORT AND BEEF IMPORT RESTRICTIONS; HOW THEY WORK.** Washington, U.S. Dept. of Agriculture, Economic Research Service, 1990, p. 38

USD-ERS briefing booklet. Each page contains a 'screen' of illustrative material, accompanied above and below by 'instructor's comments', followed by a question to the reader. The answer to each question will be found on the next page. Partial contents: Japan's geography, diet, and politics; Japan's rice policy; Japan's beef policy; United States—Japan beef agreement (Trend of the future?).

F004. Lassanyi, M.E. **JAPAN'S AGRICULTURAL MARKETING AND TRADE, JANUARY 1988–AUGUST 1990.** Beltsville, MD.: National Agricultural Library, 1990, p. 14.

Lists 150 citations from the AGRICOLA database. Citations are listed alphabetically by title; an author index is included.

F005. Paarlberg, R.L. **THE UPSIDE-DOWN WORLD OF U.S.–JAPANESE AGRICULTURAL TRADE.** *Washington Quarterly*, Vol. 13, autumn 1990, pp. 131–142.

Reviews the Japanese performance as the world's largest importer of agricultural products. In agriculture, the trade deficit that is growing is Japanese rather than American; the agricultural consumers who are benefitting are Japanese rather than American; and the agricultural producers who are benefitting are American rather than Japanese.

F006. Sanderson, F.H. (Ed.). **AGRICULTURAL PROTECTIONISM IN THE INDUSTRIALIZED WORLD**. Washington: Resources for the Future, 1990, 488 pp.

This book presents a comprehensive analysis of agricultural policies in the European Community (EC), North America, Japan, Australia, and New Zealand. It examines the economic and political forces responsible for the growth of protectionist policies and the effects of those policies on production, consumption, trade, prices, farm incomes, land values, and agricultural structures. It also assesses the costs of these policies to consumers and taxpayers as compared with their benefits to producers. Concluding chapters summarize lessons learned for domestic and trade policy.

F007. **U.S. GENERAL ACCOUNTING OFFICE.**

International trade: competition for Japan's high value agricultural market; report to congressional requesters. Mar. 30, 1990, Washington, G.A.O., 1990, p. 27. This report summarizes high value agricultural product market development activities of the nine foreign competitor countries that spend the most resources on such activities in Japan. These competitors include New Zealand, Australia, Canada, France, West Germany, the United Kingdom, the Netherlands, Italy, and Denmark. Agricultural imports from these nine countries plus the United States represented about 63 percent of all agricultural imports to Japan in 1988.

F008. Wahl, T.I., Williams, G.W. and Hayes, D.J. **THE 1988 JAPANESE BEEF MARKET ACCESS AGREEMENT: A FORECAST SIMULATION ANALYSIS.** *Agribusiness*, Vol. 5, July 1989, pp. 347–360.

This article utilizes dynamic simulation analysis to consider the likely consequences of the 1988 Japanese Beef Market Access Agreement (BMAA) on the Japanese livestock industry and beef imports. The results lead to a number of conclusions. Beef imports will increase to the new quota level in the first three years and continue increasing at about the same rate thereafter. The shift from the import quota to the import tariff in 1991 will have little effect on imports or prices. Finally, the U.S. share of increasing Japanese beef imports will increase at the expense of Australia and New Zealand.

F009. **WORLD AGRICULTURE SITUATION AND OUTLOOK REPORT**. Special Issue: Forces for change in the 1990's. Washington, U.S. Department of Agriculture, Economic Research Service, 1990, p. 76. WAS-59, June 1990.

Partial contents—Dynamics of trade negotiations, by S.L. Magiera and M. Johnson. EC 1992: economic integration and world trade effects, by W. Gardiner, S. Neff and D. Kelch. The safe food issue: new non-tariff barriers? by T. Raney and D. Kelch. Economic restructuring in the USSR and its potential impact on agricultural trade, by E.C. Cook. China's agriculture and trade: development and prospects, by F.C. Tuan. The changing structure of Japanese agricultural trade, by W. Coyle. Developing countries: changing closed systems to open ones, by D.W. Skully and T.L. Vollrath. Currency convertibility in Eastern Europe and the USSR: issues, effects, and prospects, by F. Urban.

G. FINANCE; BANKING; BUSINESS

G001. Aguayo, R. **DR. DEMING: THE AMERICAN WHO TAUGHT THE JAPANESE ABOUT QUALITY.** Lyle Stuart, 1990.
In the 1950's Deming was invited to advise Japanese business leaders on quality—thereby changed the course of Japanese industry.

G002. Ando, A. and Auerbach, A.J. **THE COST OF CAPITAL IN JAPAN: RECENT EVIDENCE AND FURTHER RESULTS.** Cambridge: National Bureau of Economic Research, 1990, 42 pp.
Continuing the research in an earlier study (LRS87-6410), this report examines the distinction between large and small Japanese firms in their cost of capital. Also provides a correction to Japanese accounting statements for unmeasured returns to land.

G003. Aoki, M. **TOWARD AN ECONOMIC MODEL OF THE JAPANESE FIRM.** *Journal of Economic Literature,* Vol. 28, Mar 1990, pp. 1–27.
Describes a model of the Japanese firm in which horizontal coordination among operating units based on knowledge sharing, rather than skill specialization, is an important internal characteristic. Aslo argues that Japanese firms depend on employee competition to achieve higher status within their hierarchies of rank as a primary incentive device. Claims that in a bank-oriented financial system, the financial and internal characteristics of Japanese firms are closely related to each other.

G004. Branford, D.F. **WHAT IS NATIONAL SAVING?: ALTERNATIVE MEASURES IN HISTORICAL AND INTERNATIONAL CONTEXT.** Cambridge: National Bureau of Economic Research, 1990, 56 pp.
Presents data on U.S. saving behavior and compares it with Japan. Sweden, and Great Britain. Argues that more attention should be paid to measures of national wealth at asset market values.

G005. Cargill, T.F. **CENTRAL BANK INDEPENDENCE AND REGULATORY RESPONSIBILITIES: THE BANK OF JAPAN AND THE FEDERAL RESERVE.** New York: Salomon Brothers Center for the Study of Financial Institutions, 1989, 80 pp.
Looks at the experience of Japan and the U.S. in investigating the relationship between central bank independence and macroeconomic performance. Also offers some insights about the most effective type of central bank involvement in the supervision and regulation of the financial system.

G006. Choy, J. **FORMER JAPANESE PUBLIC CORPORATIONS: POST-PRIVATIZATION UPDATE**. Washington: *Japanese Economic Institute*, 1990, 21 pp.

Although they have been privatized for several years, the best known Japanese public service corporations—Nippon Telegraph and Telephone Corp., Japan Railways Group, Japan Airlines Co., Ltd. and Japan Tobacco Inc.—are not free of government control. At the same time Tokyo has deregulated to varying degrees the markets that these ex-public corporations once considered their fiefdoms. Facing a newly competitive environment, these companies have responded with new services and diversification.

G007. Christelow, D.B. **U.S.–JAPAN JOINT VENTURES: WHO GAINS?** *Challenge*, Vol. 32, Nov.–Dec. 1989, pp. 39–31,34–38.

Joint ventures may bring more technology and expertise to the United States than they do to Japan, because most such partnerships are in industries in which the Japanese have a competitive advantage.

G008. Chuppe, T.M., Haworth, H.R. and Watkins, M.G. **THE SECURITIES MARKETS IN THE 1980S: A GLOBAL PERSPECTIVE.** Washington, U.S. Securities and Exchange Commission, 1989, p. 147.

This study provides an analysis of the forces shaping the internationalization of securities markets as well as a perspective on the outlook for the continuation of this process into the 1990s. The study begins with an analysis of global macroeconomic trends. This is followed by an examination of the regulatory developments in the U.S., the United Kingdom, Japan, and other countries. There is a review of significant developments in equity markets around the world.

G009. Corker, R. **WEALTH, FINANCIAL LIBERALIZATION, AND THE DEMAND FOR MONEY IN JAPAN.** *International Monetary Fund staff papers*, Vol. 37, June 1990, pp. 418–432.

Concludes that wealth effects and the opportunity cost of holding broad money can explain the developments in velocity. In the period 1986–88, these variables were strongly influenced by the rapid pace of financial liberalization in Japan.

G010. Corrigan, E.G. **TRENDS IN INTERNATIONAL BANKING IN THE UNITED STATES AND JAPAN** *Federal Reserve Bank of New York Quarterly Review*, Vol. 14, Autumn 1989, pp. 1–6.

The presence of Japanese banks in U.S. markets far exceeds the presence of U.S. banks in Japanese markets. To be specific, there are about twenty U.S. banks with a presence in Japan. In the aggregate, these banks have about $30 billion in assets—a very small market share by any measure. By contrast, there are about three dozen Japanese banks in the United States, and their aggregate banking assets amount to about $370 billion.

G011. **COUNTRY WATCH: JAPAN, THE DUSK BEFORE THE DAWN.** *Asian Finance*, Vol. 16, Aug. 1990, pp. 35–38,40–48,50–52.

Partial contents—Bank profits and capital ratios take hard knocks. Quant fad sweeps fund managers. Reciprocity vital to market reform. Warrants collapse closes a gold-mine.

G012. Cox, J. and Kriegbaum, H. **INNOVATION AND INDUSTRIAL STRENGTH IN THE UK, WEST GERMANY, UNITED STATES AND JAPAN.** London: Policy Studies Institute, 1989, 168 pp.

Looks at five different industries (mechanical engineering, programming, motor vehicles, chemicals, and textiles) to see how each employs its revenues both in times of prosperity and of decline. Studies are made of investment in research, innovation and fixed capital; of the growing expenditure on outside services; of taxes; and finally of interest rates and interest payments where money is borrowed. It is found that each technology has its own typical pattern of cash flow, which changes little over time.

G013. Curran, J.J. **JAPAN TRIES TO COOL MONEY MANIA.** *Fortune*, Vol. 123, Jan. 28, 1991, pp. 66–72,76.

Claims that for Japanese companies the era of free and easy money, unbridled expansion, and lavish market values is over. Their new world will be marked by higher interest rates, much slower growth, and plenty of unpleasant surprises. One of them may be the country's first economic slowdown in five years.

G014. Cuts, R.L. **POWER FROM THE GROUND UP: JAPAN'S LAND BUBBLE** *Harvard Business Review*, Vol. 68, May–June 1990, pp. 164–172.

Claims that the Tokyo real estate boom has created a vast "money machine" by developing massive amounts of paper assets, driving up share prices on the Tokyo Stock market, and exporting the resulting capital. The Japanese can now afford to buy whatever they want that is for sale in capital, financial, manufacturing, high-technology, knowledge-intensive, distribution, processing, and services industries anywhere in the world. And they can afford to outbid anyone else who might want it.

G015. Dore, R., Bounine-Cabale, J. and Tapiola, K. **JAPAN AT WORK: MARKETS, MANAGEMENT AND FLEXIBILITY.** Paris: Organization for Economic Co-operation and Development, 1989, 91 pp.

This analysis of the mechanisms and evolution of flexibility in Japanese labor markets examines the dynamic processes whereby workers and organizations adapt to new technologies, evolving markets and other changes. Going beyond usual notions of flexibility, the study emphasizes: the diversifying firm, the role of training and the learning environment in the firm, and the processes of redeployment of labor within the firm shows how these are facilitated by the lifetime employment commitment in Japan.

G016. Douglas, S.P. and Craig, C.S. **ACHIEVING SUCCESS IN JAPANESE CONSUMER MARKETS.** *Japan and the World Economy*, Vol. 2, No. 1, 1990, pp. 1–21.

Interviews 17 successful consumer goods firms which have penetrated Japanese markets. Identifies a number of factors responsible for their success. These (factors) centered around the creation of a strong brand or corporate image, attention to product quality and packaging, and establishment of an effective distribution and service network by fostering strong personal relations and trust with distributors.

G017. **THE ECONOMIC DYNAMICS OF AN AGEING POPULATION: A CASE OF FOUR OECD COUNTRIES.** Paris: Organization for Economic Co-operation and Development, Dept. of Economics and Statistics, 1989, 39 pp.

Alan Auerbach, Laurence Kotlikoff, Robert Hagemann, and Giuseppi Nicoletti use an overlapping generations demographic simulation model to study effects of demographic changes on national savings, wages, and public welfare costs in Japan, West Germany, Sweden, and the U.S.

G018. Elton, E.J. (Ed.) **JAPANESE CAPITAL MARKETS: ANALYSIS AND CHARACTERISTICS OF EQUITY, DEBT, AND FINANCIAL FUTURES MARKETS.** Harper and Row, 1990, ISBN 0-88730-339-0, 371 pp.

Institutional investor series in finance.

G019. Enderwick, P. **THE INTERNATIONAL COMPETITIVENESS OF JAPANESE SERVICE INDUSTRIES: A CAUSE FOR CONCERN?** *California Management Review*, Vol. 32, Summer 1990, pp. 22–37.

This article offers an assessment of the international competitiveness of Japanese service industries and examines the sources of competitive edge which have been developed within Japan. It distinguishes three groups of service industries: those where Japan currently enjoys a high degree of international competitiveness (banking, finance, and construction); those where international competitiveness is unlikely to be achieved in the foreseeable future (education, legal services, and software); and, most important, an intermediate group within which Japan's international competitiveness is rising rapidly (advertising, engineering services, real estate, and insurance). The article concludes with a number of analogies between the success of Japanese manufacturing firms and their counterparts in the service sector.

G020. Enderwick, P. **MULTINATIONAL CORPORATE RESTRUCTURING AND INTERNATIONAL COMPETITIVENESS.** *California Management Review*, Vol. 32, Fall 1989, pp. 44–58.

Compares patterns of restructuring within leading U.S. and Japanese companies since the late 1970s....In the long-term, the restructuring strategies pursued by Japanese multinationals appear to offer some significant and enduring competitive benefits. This is because the most widely adopted strategies have their principal impact on proprietary competitive assets and internationalization advantages. In contrast, the emphasis of U.S. corporations has been on overcoming locational disadvantage and restoring the conditions for competitive operation in the home market. This emphasis, while enhancing locational or comparative advantage, does little to create proprietary competitive advantages.

G021. Evans, G. **WHY IBJ COULD OUST NOMURA.** *Euromoney*, May 1989, pp. 46,48,51–52,54–55.

The Industrial Bank of Japan (IBJ) has the largest market capitalization of any company in the world. Now it's planning to use its power to become a world-class investment bank. In particular, when restrictions on corporate underwriting at home and for Japanese banks in the international markets are deregulated—probably next year—IBJ will be able to flex its muscles even more. It looks likely to squash flat the Japanese securities houses (and the likes of CSFB). Even the mighty Nomura should worry. In five years IBJ could be Japan's top underwriter. It could even head the Eurobond league tables.

G022. Fabozzi, F.J. (Ed.) **JAPANESE BOND MARKETS: AN OVERVIEW AND ANALYSIS.** Probus Pub. Co., 1990, ISBN 1-557-38112-7, 537 pp.

G023. Fallows, J. **CONTAINING JAPAN.** *Atlantic Monthly*, Vol. 263, May 1989, pp. 40–48,51–54.

Argues that it is essential that American policy-makers recognize the conflict of American and Japanese interests, because it free's us of the delusion that normal business competition will balance out whatever is unbalanced now. Asserts that this conflict arises from Japan's inability or unwillingness to restrain the one-sided and destructive expansion of its economic power. The expansion is one-sided because Japanese business does to other countries what Japan will not permit to be done to itself. It is destructive because it will lead to exactly the international ostracism that Japan most fears, because it will wreck the postwar system of free trade that has made Japan and many other nations prosperous, and because it will ultimately make the U.S.–Japanese partnership impossible to sustain.

G024. Feldman, R.A. **ROBERT A. FELDMAN ON THE INTERNATIONALIZATION OF THE YEN.** *Japan Economic Survey*, Vol. 13, Dec. 1989, pp. 6–11.

With the emergence of Japan as an economic power, some experts believe that Japanese yen is destined to be used more widely in international transactions. While this internationalism has more than one dimension, much of the discussion has centered around the potential for yen-denominated assets to be used more widely in international financial transactions. In a recent conversation with JES Editor Barbara Wanner, Robert A. Feldman, vice president of Salomon Bros., Inc., points out that Japanese financial markets have many of the characteristics needed to facilitate such internationalization, although there remain some areas of weakness compared to the United States.

G025. Fingleton, E. **EASTERN ECONOMICS.** *Atlantic Monthly*, Vol. 266, Oct. 1990, pp. 72–74,77,80–82,85.

Many of the obstacles that deter foreign companies from doing business in Japan are, it has been said, not meant to be protectionist but rather represent piecemeal responses to pleading from special interests. A revisionist school of economists takes a different view. The revisionists maintain that Japanese bureaucrats have deliberately engineered the country's retailing and housing constrictions in order to suppress consumption and enforce savings. U.S. efforts (such as the Structural Impediments Initiative) fail to understand this relationship.

G026. Foote, S.B. and W. Mitchell. **SELLING AMERICAN MEDICAL EQUIPMENT IN JAPAN.** *California Management Review*, Vol. 31, Summer 1989, pp. 146–161.

Although American sales of medical equipment to Japan have been increasing, American purchases of Japanese goods have risen even faster. It is important that this innovative industrial sector improve sales in Japan. This article discusses the unique features of Japanese public policies toward the regulation and sale of medical equipment and analyzes successful corporate strategies for increasing sales in Japan.

G027. Frankel, J.A. **JAPANESE FINANCE: A SURVEY.** Cambridge: National Bureau of Economic Research, 1989, 67 pp.

Five sets of questions puzzle observers of Japanese financial markets, particularly from the U.S. viewpoint. They concern: the apparently low corporate cost of capital, low real interest rates, high equity prices, high land prices, and the rising real yen. The paper surveys writings on these issues, in brief enough form that one can see how the questions fit together.

G028. Frankel, J.A. **THE SII OUTCOME: IN WHOSE BEST INTEREST?** *International Economy*, Vol. 4, Oct.–Nov. 1990, pp. 70–72.

Argues that what was most unusual about SII was that each side made demands that were in the interest of the other side....The U.S. government asked Japan to reform some aspects of its economy....the Japanese government asked the U.S. side to....increase its household savings rate....to try to reduce the cost of capital and to spend more on education and research.

G029. French, K.R. and Poterba, J.M. **ARE JAPANESE STOCK PRICES TOO HIGH?** Cambridge: National Bureau of Economic Research, 1990, 41 pp.

Claims that nearly half the disparity between price-earnings ratios in the U.S. and Japan is caused by differences in accounting practices with respect to consolidation of earnings from subsidiaries and depreciation of fixed assets. As for the sharp rise in Japanese stock prices in the mid-1990s, changes in required returns on equities, or in investor expectations of future growth for Japanese firms, must be invoked to explain this phenomenon.

G030. Fukushima, G. **BACK TO BUSINESS.** *Business Tokyo*, Vol. 4, July 1990, pp. 38,40–41.

Discuss U.S.–Japan trade relations. Argues that Japan is a brilliant negotiator and a formidable competitor, current U.S. efforts to change Japan are futile and ineffective. The United States needs a focused industrial policy committed to, among other things, maintaining the nation's high-tech strength. Such a policy should be administered by a single government agency of trained specialists working in close conjunction with American business.

G031. George, B.C., Stanberry, K. and Boss, M. **NEW STEPS TO PROHIBIT INSIDER TRADING IN JAPAN: A SERIOUS COMMITMENT OR SIMPLY SAVING FACE?** *Asian Thought and Society*, Vol. 15, May 1990, pp. 227–235.

Examines the social and economic attitudes in Japan which make insider trading regulations difficult to enforce, explores the historical background of the securities law, discusses the new law and recently-promulgated regulations prohibiting insider trading, and reviews the extraterritorial enforcement agreement regarding international cooperation.

G032. **THE GLOBAL ECONOMY.** *Futures*, Vol. 21, Dec. 1989, whole issue pp. 555–676.

Presents papers from a December 1988 conference on the emerging global economy, driven by rapid technological change and the failure of socialist economies. Partial contents—Driving forces and barriers to a sustainable global economy, by M. Marien. Mutual development: towards new criteria and indicators, by H. Henderson. Accountability and the debt crisis, by T. Sato. Ethical economics: a new paradigm for global justice and stewardship, by R.D. Hamrin. The paradox of development in the Middle East, by A.A. Said. Changes in economic management systems in Hungary and other East European countries, by T. Meszaros. Principles of humanistic enterprise in Japan: a new economic system of the future, by Chiaki Nakano.

G033. Haitani, K. **THE PARADOX OF JAPAN'S GROUPISM: THREAT TO FUTURE COMPETITIVENESS?** *Asian Survey*, Vol. 30, Mar. 1990, pp. 237–250.

Examines the negative side of Japan's group-oriented value system which has also brought high labor productivity, product quality, and a long-term management outlook. Claims that Japanese groupism leads to trade friction in three areas: (1) the closed nature of the Japanese market; (2) the difficulty of taking really effective measures for reducing the frictions; and (3) the emerging problem of Japanese firms' inability to integrate foreign managerial employees into their corporate hierarchies.

G034. Hale, D.D. **GLOBAL FINANCE AND THE RETREAT TO MANAGED TRADE.** *Harvard Business Review*, Vol. 68, Jan.–Feb. 1990, pp. 150–162.

Asserts that the rise of Japanese financial power and the contradictions of U.S. economic policy are weakening the competitive position of the U.S. financial services industry—one of the few sectors where the United States still regards itself as more creative, more sophisticated, and more aggressive than its foreign rivals. As a consequence, the United States may soon face the same market erosion in financial services that has afflicted its producers of machine tools, automobiles, and semiconductors.

G035. Hayashi, F. **IS JAPAN'S SAVING RATE HIGH?** *Federal Reserve Bank of Minneapolis Quarterly Review*, Vol. 13, Spring 1989, pp. 3–25.

Asserts that Japan's postwar saving rate has not been consistently higher than the U.S. rate. The Japanese rate fell from its peak in 1970 to the U.S. rate in the late 1970s, but since 1983 it has started to rise again, diverging from the U.S. rate. Claims that if the divergence is due to differences in the countries' budget deficit policies, then the rates won't converge until their budget policies do. Several conclusions are refuted by Lawrence J. Christiano in an accompanying article: Understanding Japan's saving rate: the reconstruction hypothesis.

G036. Hayashi, F. **JAPAN'S SAVING RATE: NEW DATA AND REFLECTIONS.** Cambridge: National Bureau of Economic Research, 1989, 34 pp.

This paper examines available evidence on Japan's wealth accumulation. Time-series evidence over the last one hundred years indicates that the phenomenon of extraordinary high Japanese saving rate is limited to the high-growth era of 1965–1975. Microevidence about consumption and saving by age can be more easily explained by the dynasty model than by the life-cycle hypothesis. The infinite horizon neoclassical growth model, while capable of generating the hump in the saving rate and explaining why it was preceded by rapid GNP growth in the post-war period, leaves unanswered the question of why wealth accumulation in pre-war Japan was so slow. Perhaps growth in pre-war Japan was hampered by harmful effects of misguided government policies.

G037. Healey, D. **JAPANESE CAPITAL EXPORTS AND ASIAN ECONOMIC DEVELOPMENT.** OECD Publishing, 1990, ISBN 92-64-13484-0, 256 pp.

Japan, already the world's largest donor of aid, is also uniquely positioned to help meet the investment requirements of a capital-hungry world. Challenging conventional wisdom regarding global financial imbalances, the author argues that Japan's balance of payments surplus is not unduly large relative to its ill-advised to try to reduce this surplus, as an important source of investment for development. Focusing on the Pacific-Asian region, this report looks closely at the links between trade, investment and aid, and draws lessons regarding the criteria that will likely affect Japanese overseas investment decisions in the years to come.

G038. Hector. G. **JAPAN LEARNS THE TAKEOVER GAME.** *Fortune,* Vol. 120, July 31, 1989, pp. 121,124,128.

Buyers still think long-term, but they are moving faster, luring U.S. managers with lucrative contracts, and even walking away from overpriced deals.

G039. Helleiner, Eric. **MONEY AND INFLUENCE: JAPANESE POWER IN THE INTERNATIONAL MONETARY AND FINANCIAL SYSTEM.** *Millennium,* Vol. 18, Winter 1989, pp. 343–358.

Examines the growing power of Japan in the international financial system, concentrating on two separate developments: Japan's emergence as a creditor nation and the internationalization of the Japanese financial system. Each of these can be seen to have brought a different kind of power to the Japanese state.

G040. Holden, T. **THE TOKYO STOCK MARKET AND HOW ITS SWINGS AFFECT YOU.** *Business Week,* No. 3145, Feb. 12, 1990, pp. 74–79,82–84.

Profiles the rapid rise of the Tokyo Stock Exchange to become the largest stock market in the world. Describes the differences between the Tokyo and U.S. markets. Concludes that Japan's buying machine may already be revving up again. But the quick riches of 1989 probably won't return. Includes two companion articles, How Real Estate Pumps Up Japanese Stocks, and When Japan gets the Gitters, the World Trembles.

G041. Holloway, N. **JAPAN: FINANCE and INVESTMENT.** *Far Eastern Economic Review,* Vol. 146, Dec. 14, 1989, pp. 49–82 passim p. 16.

Looks at changes in Japan's financial markets, where foreign firms are beginning to make money at least in securities trading. For foreign financial institutions, fund management is the final frontier in Japan, in the sense that the walls surrounding the insurance, banking and securities industries have already been breached. Asset management is the last bastion of financial exclusivism.

G042. Howard, R. **CAN SMALL BUSINESS HELP COUNTRIES COMPETE?** *Harvard Business Review,* Vol. 68, Nov.–Dec. 1990, pp. 88–90,94,96–97,100,102–103.

Addresses the role of small business in achieving competitive success. Claims that the small manufacturing sector in the United States lags behind that of other major industrial nations. Ironically, while many in the United

States have been celebrating small business, other countries—in particular, Japan and West Germany—have been using public policy to make small manufacturing a powerful asset of international competition.

G043. Hurst, G.C. **SAYING "NO" TO AMERICA: THE MORITA-ISHIHARA CRITIQUE OF THE U.S.** Indianapolis: Universities Field Staff International, 1989, 14 pp.

Some of the reaction from public figures in the US suggests that they have either misread the book or read more into it than there is ....The book is valuable, in fact, on several counts. First, it points out the reality of economic competition—now and for the foreseeable future; America is losing economic ground to Japan less because of the latter's unfair business practices than because of US inefficiencies.

G044. Imai, K. **THE LEGITIMACY OF JAPAN'S CORPORATE GROUPS.** *Economic Eye*, Vol. 11, autumn 1990, pp. 16–22.

In many foreign eyes, Japan's keiretsu, or corporate groups, epitomize an economic system that seems closed and peculiar. There can be no doubt that the cross-holdings of shares within these groups shut out hostile raiders, but in other respects the keiretsu are far more open than is often presumed. Their network-style organization, moreover, is ideally suited to the modern market and to technological innovation. Now they must reform outmoded practices, attract foreign participants, and evolve into global corporate networks.

G045. Imhof, J.F., Jr. **THE PATHOLOGY OF INSIDER TRADING AND JAPAN'S AMENDED SECURITIES EXCHANGE LAW.** *Syracuse Journal of International Law and Commerce*, Vol. 16, Spring 1990, pp. 235–270.

Note examines insider trading regulation in Japan, including new legal provisions adopted in 1989. Claims that the failure of insider trading regulation in Japan is the product of social acceptance, traditional business structure, and the political self-interest.

G046. **INDUSTRIAL DEVELOPMENT AND FACTOR ENDOWMENTS IN EAST AND SOUTHEAST ASIA.** *Developing Economies*, Vol. 27, Dec. 1989, whole issue, pp. 309–405.

Contents—Structure and growth of an open dual economy: examining industrial policy, by M. Ohyama. A model of dual-industrial development in a semi-industrial country, by Y. Kubo. A note on the dual-industrial growth and learning effects, by K. Ohno. The dual-industrial growth in Prewar Japan, by T. Yanagihara. A test of the dual-industrial growth hypothesis: the case of the Philippines and Thailand, by H. Yokoyama and S. Itoga. Factor abundance in East and Southeast Asian countries: an empirical study with Leontief's and Leamer's formulas, by H. Yokoyama, K. Ohno, S. Itoga and H. Imaoka. Japanese corporate employment and personnel systems and their transfer to Japanese affiliates in Asia, by H. Imaoka. Export-led industrialization and the Dutch disease, by H. Yokoyama.

G047. **INSIDE JAPAN'S M&A: THE PLAYERS AND THEIR SECRETS.** *Business Tokyo*, Vol. 3, Nov. 1989, pp. 18,20–24.

Claims that as Japan gears up for even greater global expansion, more Japanese executives are being sold on the idea that M&A is the sensible way to expand or diversify their businesses and that U.S. companies are cheap and available. Offers an insight into the top American and Japanese advisors who are planning the big corporate takeovers.

G048. Isenstein, H. **WILL U.S. TOBACCO GO UP IN SMOKE?** *Tokyo Business Today*, May 1989, pp. 50–51.

Liberalization of the Japanese cigarette market prompted a rapid growth in market shares of foreign tobacco companies. But aggressive television advertising has caused a backlash.

G049. Itoh, H. **JAPAN'S EMERGING ROLE AS AN IMPORT ABSORBER.** *Economic Eye*, Vol. 10, Winter 1989, pp. 28–31.

The import boom, says the 1989 white paper on trade, is here to stay. Manufacturers have found that they can make money by using more imported parts and selling imported items along with their own merchandise. Distributors have also jumped on the import bandwagon and seem especially interested in made-to-order products. Here one of the white paper's authors reviews these and other trends in trade. While continuing to boost imports, Japan must take the lead in tackling new trade issues.

G050. Itoh, M. **WORLD ECONOMIC CRISIS AND JAPANESE CAPITALISM.** St. Martins Pr., 1990, ISBN 0-312-03148-3, (approx) 264 pp.

G051. **JAPAN'S EXTERNAL ECONOMIC RELATIONS: JAPANESE PERSPECTIVES.** *Annals of the American Academy of Political and Social Science*, Vol. 513, Jan. 1991, whole issue, p. 210.

Partial contents—Japan as a world economic power, by M. Shinohara. Japan's role in Asia–Pacific cooperation, by S. Okita. Japan's defense strategy, by A. Iriye. Japan's foreign direct investment, by R. Komiya and R. Wakasugi. Japanese economic cooperation, by Y. Kosai and K. Matsuyama. Japan's resource imports, by K. Sato. The overseas strategies of Japanese corporations, by M. Trevor. The employment of foreign labor in Japan, by H. Shimada. Japan: model society of the future? by M. Sumiya.

G052. **JAPAN'S FINANCIAL MARKETS.** *International Economy*, Vol. 3, July–Aug. 1989, pp. 34,36–40,42–51.

In a series of articles, claims that liberalization of Japan's financial markets has still left huge cultural and financial barriers to foreign participation. Claims that some aspects of Japan's regulatory system, however, support global financial stability and the dollar's international status as a key currency, and that deregulation might lead to interest rate gyrations and mediocre banking supervision that characterized America in the 1980s.

G053. Johsen, T. and Noriko, H. **AN ECONOMIC METAMORPHOSIS FOR JAPAN?** *Japan Quarterly*, Vol. 37, July–Sept. 1990, pp. 260–264,266–269.

Describes the likely economic impact of declining stock and bond prices and the value of the yen which have occurred in 1990. Japan's money-soaked expansion, born out of unprecedented excess liquidity and low interest rates, is now confronting a series of significant changes. The very forces at work behind the extremely heated economy have by now been stretched so far that they have little choice but to head toward self-destruction.

G054. Jones, R.S. **POLITICAL ECONOMY OF JAPAN'S AGRICULTURAL POLICIES.** *World Economy*, Vol. 12, Mar. 1989, pp. 29–38.

Observes that Japan's farm-support programs have created an inefficient agricultural sector dominated by part-time farming on small pieces of land. The disappointing productivity gains in the agricultural sector have required increasing transfers from consumers and taxpayers to boost farm incomes and achieve the goal of income parity. Highly restrictive trade barriers have been employed to maintain the resulting gap between domestic and international prices. Concludes that the key to reforming Japan's agricultural sector is land consolidation to enable farmers to increase their scale of operation and reduce production costs.

G055. Kang, T.W. **GAISHI: THE FOREIGN COMPANY IN JAPAN.** BasicBooks, 1990, 279 pp.

Most books about doing business in Japan are written by Westerners—by academics, consultants, and executives concerned with helping foreign companies to succeed in a difficult environment. *Gaishi*, by contrast, is an authoritative insider's account: the work of a senior Korean executive fluent in both Japanese and English, with extensive business experience in both the United States and Japan. The book shows how understanding Japan's very different business culture can help managers develop more effective strategies for every aspect of corporate activity, whether it be product design, sales, recruitment, training, or partnering.

G056. Katayama, R. and Ribeiro, J. **MOTOROLA'S ON THE LINE: WILL JAPAN PICK UP?** *Business Tokyo*, Vol. 4, Sept. 1990, pp. 36–41.

Profiles Motorola's efforts in penetrating the Japanese telecommunications market. Details the Japanese bureaucratic resistance to imports of American telecommunications equipment during a period when Japanese telecommunications exports to the U.S. soared.

G057. Kester, W.C. **JAPANESE TAKEOVERS: THE GLOBAL CONTEST FOR CORPORATE CONTROL.** Harvard Univ. Press, 1990, 300 pp.

G058. Kirslov, J. **HOW DOES THE JAPANESE INDUSTRIAL RELATIONS SYSTEM DIFFER?** *Labor Law Journal*, Vol. 40, June 1989, pp. 338–346.

Concludes that Japan is a nation with little overt industrial conflict, as compared with nations that have troubled industrial relations. It does not, however, compare so favorably with several European nations that are noted for peaceful labor relations. What is, however, truly distinctive and undoubtedly worthy of emulation is the Japanese way of sharing information and obtaining consensus.

G059. Koo, R. **NEEDED: AN AMERICAN CORPORATE PERESTROIKA.** *International Economy*, Vol. 4, Feb.–Mar. 1990, pp. 59–61.

A leading Japanese economist argues that U.S. companies operate like the Soviet economy. Argues that everyone in Japanese firms is expected to think for the firm, while only the top few in U.S. corporations are expected to do the same (and even fewer in the Soviet economy). The U.S. has 200 million people, but if only one-tenth are expected to think while the others are simply asked to follow, the total number of working brain cells may still be less than that in Japan with 100 million people....the U.S. can ill afford to forget the lessons of Soviet failure.

G060. Lee. P. **RESTRUCTURING,** *Japanese-style Euromoney,* Mar. 1990, pp. 31–34,36.

Japan looks ripe for a wave of corporate restructuring. Inefficiencies abound. There is potential for rationalization, cost-cutting, mergers, acquisitions and divestitures—and lucrative advisory fees.

G061. Levy, S.M. **JAPANESE CONSTRUCTION: AN AMERICAN PERSPECTIVE.** New York: Van Nostrand Reinhold, 1990, 413 pp.

Contents.—The Japanese presence in the United States today.—The construction industry in Japan.—The functioning construction company.—Marketing—domestically and overseas.—Estimating, bidding, cost and quality control.—The contract documents.—The construction process.—Unionism in Japan and the construction unions.—Movers and shakers—robots and seismics.—Construction techniques.—Research and development.—Competing with the Japanese.

G062. Lincoln, J.R. **EMPLOYEE WORK ATTITUDES AND MANAGEMENT PRACTICE IN THE U.S. AND JAPAN: EVIDENCE FROM A LARGE COMPARATIVE SURVEY.** *California Management Review,* Vol. 32, Fall 1989, pp. 89–106.

Surveys 106 Japanese and U.S. factories and 8,302 of their employees on how work attitudes and motivation differ between Japanese and U.S. employees and whether management practice and organizational design can account for those differences. The article concludes that practices such as quality circles, the ringi system, centralized authority combined with de facto participation, employee services, seniority compensation, and enterprise unions do, in fact, help to explain the 'commitment gap' that divides the Japanese from the U.S. manufacturing workforce. When these and similar practices appear in U.S. factories, similar positive changes in employee work attitudes result.

G063. Macey, J. and Kanda, H. **THE STOCK EXCHANGE AS A FIRM: THE EMERGENCE OF CLOSE SUBSTITUTES FOR THE NEW YORK AND TOKYO STOCK EXCHANGES.** *Cornell Law Review,* Vol. 75, July 1990, pp. 1007–1052.

Article asserts that market reform in the form of new regulation is doomed to failure until the economic functions of organized exchanges are better understood. Of particular importance are the mechanisms by which prices are set within the exchanges, and the degree of competition that exchanges face for the various services they offer. Thus the purpose of this Article is to articulate the economic underpinnings of organized stock exchanges. Focuses on differences between the U.S. and Japanese exchanges.

G064. March, R.M. **NO-NOS IN NEGOTIATING WITH THE JAPANESE.** *Across the Board,* Vol. 26, Apr. 1989, pp. 44–51.

Excerpts from Robert March's book, "The Japanese Negotiator," a case study that shows the dos and don'ts in business negotiations with a Japanese firm.

G065. **MARKETS IN JAPAN FOR U.S. LUMBER PRODUCTS.** *Construction Review*, Vol. 35, July–Aug. 1989, pp. 3–13.

This article is excerpted from a report prepared by the Office of Forest Products and Domestic Construction of the International Trade Administration. The full 218-page report can be purchased from the U.S. Government Printing Office and is entitled "The Japanese Solid Wood Products Market: Profile and Outlook."

G066. McCauley, R.N. and Zimmer, S.A. **EXPLAINING INTERNATIONAL DIFFERENCES IN THE COST OF CAPITAL.** *Federal Reserve Bank of New York Quarterly Review*, Vol. 14, Summer 1989, pp. 7–28.

Estimates the cost of capital for corporations in the United States, Japan, Germany, and Britain in the period 1977–88 and finds that the United States and Britain labor under a decided disadvantage in relation to the other two economies.

G067. McKinney, J.A. **DEGREE OF ACCESS TO THE JAPANESE MARKET 1979 VS. 1986.** Columbia Journal of World Business, Vol. 24, Summer 1989, pp. 53–59.

This article compares the results of a 1979 survey of U.S. firms operating in Japan with the results of a similar 1986 survey. Questions related to tariff and non-tariff trade barriers are analyzed. Results indicate that access to the Japanese market has definitely increased between 1979 and 1986, although some problem areas remain.

G068. Meyers, W. **HOW AMERICA IS LOSING CONTROL OVER INTEREST RATES.** *Institutional Investor*, Vol. 24, Apr. 1990, pp. 49–54.

Rising rates in Germany and Japan are forcing the Fed's hand. If the U.S. is to attract overseas buyers for Treasury debt, domestic policies may have to take a backseat.

G069. **MITSUI-TAIYO KOBE MERGER CREATES A MEGABANK.** *Tokyo Business Today*, Vol. 57, Oct. 1989, pp. 16–21.

Discuses the merger of two Japanese banks which will create the second largest bank in the world.

G070. Miyohei, S. **JAPAN'S ROLE IN A CHANGING WORLD ECONOMY.** *Japan Echo*, Vol. 17, Spring 1990, pp. 17–28.

Discusses trends likely to prevail in the world economy as we enter the twenty-first century, focusing on the U.S., Asia, and the Communist nations. Addresses the issue of Japan's lopsided external surplus and the potential uses of those funds as development assistance.

G071. Morgan, J.C. and Morgan, J.J. **CRACKING THE JAPANESE MARKET: STRATEGIES FOR SUCCESS IN THE NEW GLOBAL ECONOMY.** Free Press, 1990, ISBN 0-02-921691-5, 288 pp.

G072. Murphy, R.T. **POWER WITHOUT PURPOSE: THE CRISIS OF JAPAN'S GLOBAL FINANCIAL DOMINANCE.** *Harvard Business Review*, Vol. 67, Mar.–Apr. 1989, pp. 71–94.

Draws a picture of Japan as the world's leading financial power, but one which lacks the ideology and political commitment necessary to fulfill the obligations that go with financial power. Claims that Japan will not sacrifice its own interests for the interests of the global financial system, pointing to Japan's reluctance to use the yen as a global reserve currency or to act as a global lender of last resort. Also faults Japan for its closed trading system. Includes companion article by Alan M. Webber featuring an interview with Yasuhiro Nakasone.

G073. Nagourney, S.H. **YEN FOR TROUBLE: WHAT'S WRONG WITH JAPAN'S STOCK MARKET IS JAPAN.** *Barron's*, Vol. 70, Mar. 26, 1990, pp. 13–16,18,20,22.

Claims that the plunge in Tokyo's stock market since the beginning of 1990 is rooted in more than the gross imbalance between the earnings yields on stocks and the yield on bonds. Maintains that Japan's policy of cultivating one-way trade has created more yen than the economy can absorb. Policies have discouraged consumption by means of high-priced consumer goods, in effect forcing consumer income into savings and, in the process, vastly inflating financial and property assets. Includes accompanying articles by Daniel J. Kreps (Behind the bamboo curtain: new rules reveal woes of Japanese banks) and by Edward A. Wyatt (Nixing the Nikkee: there are more ways to short Tokyo).

G074. Neff, R. and Magnusson, P. **RETHINKING JAPAN: THE NEW, HARDER LINE TOWARD TOKYO.** *Business Week*, No. 3118, Aug. 7, 1989, pp. 44,46–52.

A growing cadre at the highest levels of U.S. government business, and academe is discarding the hope that the Japanese will ever subscribe to free-market rules. If they won't grown more like us, the feelings goes, maybe we can become more like them. Import restrictions and managed trade, the revisionists assert, are games two can play. Includes a Business Week/Harris poll of what 1,250 adult Americans think of Japan Inc.

G075. Nelson, S.C. **SELLING FROM THE UNITED STATES TO JAPAN: REPRESENTATION, SALES AND DISTRIBUTION AGREEMENTS WITH JAPANESE BUSINESSES.** *International Quarterly*, Vol. 2, July 1990, pp. 31–50.

Concludes that the appointment of distributors, commission agents, and sale representatives in Japan raises a number of commercial issues peculiar to the Japanese market and some legal issues involving the application of extensive Japanese law and governmental regulations. A careful examination of the law and skillful draftsmanship of the agreement establishing a business relationship can prevent many potential surprises, disputes and loss of profits.

G076. Nester, W. **JAPAN'S CORPORATE MIRACLE: IDEALS AND REALITIES AT HOME AND ABROAD.** *Asian Profile*, Vol. 17, Dec. 1989, pp. 497–511.

States that the most important factor underlying the Japanese miracle has been the ability of the Japanese government, LDP, and corporate world to work together since the early 1950s to create and implement rational industrial policies that target strategic industries for development and fuel growth rates double the average of their democratic industrial rivals. Rational industrial policies are the major reason for Japan's transformation into the world's most dynamic economic superpower.

G077. Nishikawa, K. **WHY JAPANESE CONSUMER GROUPS OPPOSE MARKET OPENING MEASURES.** *Tokyo Business Today,* Vol. 58, Mar. 1990, pp. 40–43.

Describes the historical background of Japan's consumer organizations and looks into why these groups tend to oppose trade liberalization. Asserts that there appears to be a belief among Japanese consumer groups that unfettered competition is not a desirable model, and this results in opposition to market liberalization. In this sense, the Japanese consumer movement has failed to mature and is being left behind the country's general move toward modernization.

G078. Normile, D. **THE HONEYMOON IS OVER.** *Business Tokyo,* Vol. 3, Mar. 1989, pp. 12–15.

Claims that Japanese construction firms are facing a number of challenges in expanding their U.S. presence: they have not been able to attract American clients, their Japanese clients are growing more confident about their ability to deal with American contractors, and the fixed hierarchical structure of the domestic Japanese construction market may be shaken by the competition overseas.

G079. Peterson, P.G. **JAPANESE MERGERS AND ACQUISITIONS IN AMERICA: THE DEALS AND THE DEALMAKERS.** *Japan and the World Economy,* Vol. 2, No. 1, 1990, pp. 91–106.

Argues that Americans should not be so obsessed with foreigners purchasing U.S. assets and should face the competitiveness debate directly. Also outlines several constructive steps Japan should take to open up its markets.

G080. Pickens, T.B. **T. BOONE'S BONE TO PICK.** *International Economy,* Vol. 3, Sept.–Oct. 1989, pp. 88–90.

When it comes to foreign investors, the Japanese are snobs, says America's corporate raider.

G081. Quinn, D.P. and Jacobson, R. **INDUSTRIAL POLICY THROUGH THE RESTRICTION OF CAPITAL FLOWS: A TEST OF SEVERAL CLAIMS MADE ABOUT INDUSTRIAL POLICY.** *American Journal of Political Science,* Vol. 33, Aug. 1989, pp. 700–736.

The authors examine the extent and effect of an interest rate-based industrial policy in Japan, France, Great Britain, and West Germany while using the United States as a control case. They argue that some governments have undertaken industrial policies that achieve a 'below-competitive market' interest rate, thereby allowing the redirection of financial flows to firms in the form of cheaper capital...They find that only France under the Socialists succeeded in positively affecting economic activity through this type of industrial policy, and that Britain prior to Thatcher's election demonstrated ineffective policies. Some evidence also indicates that Japan's industrial policies were less effective than previously believed.

G082. Rapoport, C. **NOW JAPAN IS PLUNGING INTO OIL.** *Fortune,* Vol. 110, Mar. 13, 1989, pp. 124–126.

No longer content merely to import crude, the Japanese are starting to explore, produce, and buy large reserves. As they say, 'It's bargain basement time for us.'

G083. Rapoport, C. **READY, SET, SELL—JAPAN IS BUYING.** *Fortune*, Vol. 120, Sept. 11, 1989, pp. 159–160,162,164.

Describes a retailing revolution in Japan as import restrictions and complicated distribution networks are breaking down and as giant discounters edge aside small family shops.

G084. Rapoport, C. **TOUGH TIMES FOR JAPAN'S BANKS.** *Fortune*, Vol. 122, July 16, 1990, pp. 66–69.

Once they seemed on the verge of taking over the world. Now the juggernaut is slowing down. Competitors can breathe easier, but borrowers should expect to pay more.

G085. Rapoport, C. **YOU CAN MAKE MONEY IN JAPAN.** *Fortune*, Vol. 121, Feb. 12, 1990, pp. 85,88,90,92.

Claim that years of U.S. pressure are beginning to pay off for American companies trying to break into the Japanese market. U.S. companies are starting to take market share not only in the consumer products shown on these pages, but also in semiconductors and financial services.

G086. Reich, M.R. **WHY THE JAPANESE DON'T EXPORT MORE PHARMACEUTICALS: HEALTH POLICY AS INDUSTRIAL POLICY.** *California Management Review*, Vol. 32, Winter 1990, pp. 124–150.

Contends that the Japanese pharmaceutical industry has been nurtured and promoted through a highly regulated market with government-set prices, where health policy has served as implicit industrial policy. Using the model of political economy, argues that competitive successes in Japan have resulted neither from bureaucratic guidance nor from market forces, but rather from political structuring of the economy.

G087. **THE RESTRUCTURING OF THE JAPANESE FINANCIAL SERVICES INDUSTRY.** Association of the Bar of the City of New York, Committee on Asian Affairs. Record of the Association of the Bar of the City of New York, Vol. 45, Mar 1990, pp. 194–213.

Article summarizes recent developments in the restructuring of the Japanese financial services industry. Focuses on activities of the Financial Systems Research Council which is considering five proposals for the restructuring of the Japanese banking industry and the entry of banks into securities underwriting and brokerage activities.

G088. Ribeiro, J. **THEY CAME, THEY SAY, THE PROFITED.** *Business Tokyo*, Vol. 3, Feb. 1989, pp. 23–29.

Describes the experiences of five foreign companies that have successfully broken into the Japanese market.

G089. Rosen, D. **BROADCASTING IN THE PUBLIC INTEREST: LESSONS FROM JAPAN.** *Constitutional Commentary*, Vol. 7, Winter 1990, pp. 35–59.

Examines Japanese public broadcasting with a focus on its finance. Makes comparisons between broadcasting in the U.S. and Japan. Suggests that the United States charge a spectrum free on commercial broadcasters and use some of the revenue to support public broadcasting.

G090. Royama, S. **A BANKING GOLIATH IS BORN: BAD NEWS FOR THE PUBLIC?** *Economic Eye*, Vol. 10, Winter 1989, pp. 22–23.

When the Mitsui and Taiyo Kobe banks announced that they would merge, nearly everybody welcomed the move. They judged that the strengths of each institution would complement each other, and they were happy to see another Japanese name at the top of the world's bank rankings. But in today's global banking, where market and country risks are rising, bigger is not necessarily better. In the upcoming shakeout in the financial sector, mergers must be planned with the public good in mind.

G091. Rubenstein, J.M. **JAPANESE MOTOR VEHICLE PRODUCERS IN THE U.S.A.: WHERE AND WHY.** *Focus*, Vol. 40, Summer 1990, pp. 7–11.

Relates the trend of the 1970s and 1980s of Japanese car makers invading the American automobile market. Observes that the old days of foreign and domestic competition are gone and are now replaced by a complex web of global relationships.

G092. Russell, D. **ENTERING THE INVESTMENT DECADE.** *Business Tokyo*, Vol. 4, Jan. 1990, pp. 26–30.

Looks at the mergers and acquisitions (M and A) market in Japan and the role of cross-border M and A deals in Japanese business strategy. Claims that in two decades of Japanese acquisitions of U.S. companies, there has not been a single case of a truly hostile takeover.

G093. Russell, D. **HOW THE JAPANESE TURN DIRT INTO GOLD.** *Business Tokyo*, Vol. 4, Aug. 1990, pp. 20–25.

Investigates the unique character of Japan's real estate market in which even a little land equals a tremendous amount of capital. Looks at how this sets the stage for a continuing wave of acquisitions of prime U.S. properties.

G094. Sakai, K. **THE FEUDAL WORLD OF JAPANESE MANUFACTURING.** *Harvard Business Review*, Vol. 68, Nov.–Dec. 1990, pp. 38–40,42,44–45,48–49.

Describes Japan's large industrial conglomerates as trading companies. Rather than design and manufacture their own goods, they actually coordinate a complex design and manufacturing process that involves thousands of smaller companies. Claims that foreign companies can take advantage of this system by learning the process of subcontracting.

G095. Samuelson, R.J. **THE WAR THAT NEVER WAS.** *International Economy*, Vol. 3, May–June 1989, pp. 80,82–86.

Asserts that the U.S. and Japanese economies have grown more interdependent, and mutual political interests around the world are rising. A genuine economic war would hurt everyone. It would mean new trade or investment restrictions and a climate that made both Americans and Japanese fearful of doing business in the other country. Includes companion article by Senator Max Baucus on strategies to open the Japanese market.

G096. Sawano, N. **CONSUMER CREDIT AND LAW IN JAPAN.** *Personal Finance Law Quarterly Report*, Vol. 43, Summer 1989, pp. 185–189.

G097. Sayle, M. **AXIS, LTD.** *New Republic*, Vol. 200, June 5, 1989, pp. 22–24,26–27.

Examines Japan's and Germany's current economic status and status in the world market.

G098. Schmiegelow, H. and Schmiegelow, M. **HOW JAPAN AFFECTS THE INTERNATIONAL SYSTEM.** *International Organization*, Vol. 44, autumn 1990, pp. 553–588.

Reviews the attempts of mainstream economic and international relations theory to explain Japan's dramatic rise in power and its influence in the international system. Argues that the observable impact of Japan's economic performance on the international system, however it may be measured in the end, strikingly demonstrates the epistemological weaknesses of mainstream economic theory and international relations theory.

G099. **SEEKING A NEW ROLE.** *Far Eastern Economic Review*, Vol. 144, June 8, 1989, pp. 50–90 passim (21 p.).

In a series of articles, claims that "the new-found interest of Japanese bureaucrats and businessmen in East Asian economic integration seems to be partly a reflection of the fact that the region has rapidly been growing more cohesive anyway. Describes the rapid growth of intra-regional trade and investment as an important indicator of increasing economic integration.

G100. Sender, H. **DRAWING THE LINE ON DEREGULATION.** *Institutional Investor*, Vol. 23, Nov. 1989, pp. 219–220,222–223,226,230.

The reform push may look convincing, but the Ministry of Finance's zeal for order will prevent Japan from ever embracing Western-style financial markets.

G101. Sender, H. **JAPAN'S NOT-SO-MIGHTY BANKS.** *Institutional Investor*, Vol. 24, Nov. 1990, pp. 130–132,135–136,138,141–142.

Claims that Japan's smaller banks are facing serious capital shortages. Some have lost money on bad loans; many more have squandered funds on poorly timed securities investments. At the upper level, the city banks, the giants of the Japanese financial system, are systematically shrinking themselves.

G102. Shale, T. **THE GLOBAL AMBITIONS OF NIPPON LIFE.** *Euromoney*, Dec. 1989, pp. 36–38,40.

Nippon Life Insurance has launched an attack on Japan's Ministry of Finance and Japanese banks and securities houses. When it's defeated them—and won for itself the underwriting powers and other freedoms it seeks—the world's largest insurance company proposes to assault the international banking and securities markets.

G103. Shale, T. **REAWAKENING THE SLEEPING GIANT.** *Euromoney*, Nov. 1990, pp. 14,16–18,20–23.

Claims that the recent wave of corporate mergers in Japan will also continue in the 1990s. Mega-companies are going to emerge out of what are disparate groups of companies held together by cross-shareholding arrangements.

G104. Shoven, J.B. **THE JAPANESE TAX REFORM AND THE EFFECTIVE RATE OF TAX ON JAPANESE CORPORATE INVESTMENTS.** *In Tax Policy and* *the Economy*, Vol. 3 (Summers, L.H., editor), 1989, pp. 97–115, MIT Press, Cambridge, MA.

This paper presents a brief summary of the Japanese income tax system and the changes in it that have been enacted or proposed. It also discusses and evaluates the pressures for reform, both domestic and international. Finally, the paper looks at how the taxation of capital income in Japan has changed since 1980 and how it compares to the U.S. taxation of capital income after our 1986 tax reform. One major finding of the paper is that the effective marginal tax rates on corporate capital income in Japan has increased sharply since 1980, from roughly 5 percent to about 32 percent.

G105. Smith, L. **FEAR AND LOATHING OF JAPAN.** *Fortune*, Vol. 121, Feb. 26, 1990, pp. 50–53,56,58,60.

Claims that Japan bashing has been going on for a decade or so, but lately the intensity has reached stunning proportions. Contends that Japan is clearly not an enemy and that the U.S. has contributed to the problem with bad habits of its own, such as saving too little and allowing large portions of American business to grow uncompetitive.

G106. **SPECIAL ISSUE: COMPETITION ISSUES AND POLICIES. A GLOBAL SURVEY.** *Antitrust Bulletin*, Vol. 34, Fall 1989, whole issue, pp. 451–710.

Includes the legal cartels of Japan, by T. Nakazawa and L.W. Weiss.

G107. Sterling, W.P. **THE LEVERAGING OF JAPAN.** *International Economy*, Vol. 3, May–June 1989, pp. 68–74.

Claims that understanding the mechanics of real estate investment in Japan helps to explain how that country has become the world's most important creditor nation and single largest capital market. Concludes that a weakening of Japanese asset prices triggered by higher interest rates could lead to a substantial reduction in Japan's capital outflow.

G108. Stokes, B. **PRESSURES BACK HOME.** *National Journal*, Vol. 21, Feb. 4, 1989, pp. 286–291.

Discusses pressures agricultural negotiators from the U.S., EC, and Japan are expected to feel at the upcoming Uruguay Round of trade talks in Geneva. Domestic farm policy reforms are sought by budget-conscious national governments, but farm lobbies resist changes in support payments. Describes suggested U.S. policy reforms of decoupling and 'tariffication.'

G109. **STRUGGLING AGAINST THE TIDE.** *Forbes*, Vol. 146, Nov. 12, 1990, pp. 312–314,318,320.

Profiles three U.S. machine tool companies, Bodine Corp., Monarch Machine Tool, and Elox and how they have managed to stay competitive with the Japanese machine tool industry.

G110. Szirami, A. and Pilat, D. **COMPARISONS OF PURCHASING POWER, REAL OUTPUT AND LABOR PRODUCTIVITY IN MANUFACTURING IN JAPAN, SOUTH KOREA AND THE U.S.A., 1975–85.** *Review of Income and Wealth*, Vol. 36, Mar. 1990, pp. 1–31.

Concludes that value added per hour worked in Japanese manufacturing increased from 54 percent of the U.S. level in 1975 to 76 percent in 1985. In certain important branches such as electrical machinery, metal products and machinery and transport equipment, productivity leadership shifted to Japan. In South Korea, labor productivity in manufacturing increased rapidly from 1975 to 1985, both in absolute terms and relative to the U.S.A. Nevertheless, in 1985 value added per hour worked was only 14 percent of the U.S. level. Accompanied by two IBM-PC compatible diskettes containing statistical tables, shelved in the SDI loan collection.

G111. Tateisi, K. **RENEWING THE VENTURE SPIRIT.** *Across the Board*, Vol. 26, Nov. 1989, pp. 47–55.

An 89-year-old Japanese entrepreneur explains how he cured 'big-business syndrome' in his company, a pioneer in the development of controls for automation. Identifies symptoms of the syndrome as a highly centralized and swollen bureaucracy, a proliferation of special forms and permits to handle routine decisions, increasing numbers of meetings to reach decisions, and transfer of problems between departments. Excerpted from the author's book: The Eternal Venture Spirit: an Executive's Practical Philosophy.

G112. **TAX REFORM 1989: WINNERS AND LOWERS (IN JAPAN).** *Economic Eye*, Vol. 10, Spring 1989, pp. 23–26.

The tax reform package that the ruling Liberal Democratic Party rammed through the National Diet in late-1988 should bring tax relief to most categories of households while enhancing revenues through a value-added tax. Calculations made by economics in the Forum for Policy Innovation suggest, however, that households in the lowest income brackets will pay more taxes. Well-off single-income families look to reap the greatest benefits. The writers urge revisions and refinements to the tax package to provide relief to low-income families.

G113. Tokunaga, T. Blakeway-Phillips, M. and Aitken, R. **ABREAST OF THE TREND.** *Banker*, Vol. 139, Oct. 1989, pp. 18,20–21,23.

Looks at the work of bank auditors in Japan, the U.S., and the Persian Gulf States.

G114. **TOKYO FINANCIAL MARKETS, SUMMER 1989.** *Japan Economic Journal*, Vol. 27, Summer 1989, suppl., whole issue, p. 36.

Contents—Views on financial reform. Financial futures market. Stock options market. Insider trading. Money market. New short-term prime rate. Forex market. Stock market. Individual investors. Japan's stock prices. Bond market. Life insurance companies. Bank of Japan. Trading center. Interview with Y.L. Itai, James Capel Pacific Ltd. Background data.

G115. **TOP 200 FOREIGN AFFILIATED CORPORATIONS (IN JAPAN).** *Tokyo Business Today*, July 1989, pp. 20–24.

G116. Uchida, M. **TOSHIBA BOUNCES BACK.** *Tokyo Business Today*, June 1989, pp. 14–19.

After raising Washington's ire for illegal trading with Moscow, Toshiba has rebounded with an extraordinary program of 'strategic management,' massive capital investment into semiconductors, and is striving to become world information industry leader.

G117. Trevor, M. **THE OVERSEAS STRATEGIES OF JAPANESE CORPORATIONS.** *Annals of the American Academy of Political and Social Science,* Vol. 513, Jan. 1991, pp. 90–101.

Claims that the factors behind the overseas spread of Japanese corporations differ from the American multinational spread of the 1950s. Internationalization means more business, but Japanese managers fear the dilution of systems used so effectively at home. The companies therefore face problems, especially in the internationalization of management.

G118. Uchida, T. **JAPAN AND THE ARAB WORLD: AN ECONOMIC PERSPECTIVE.** *American–Arab Affairs,* No. 32, Spring 1990, pp. 27–42.

Spokesman for Japan's Ministry of Foreign Affairs describes trade and investment relations between Japan and the Middle East, including levels of official development assistance. Includes accompanying articles by Ryozo Kato (Japan's political role in the Middle East, past and present) and by Michael Collins and Julia Ackerman (The United States, Japan, and the Gulf: common interests, potential competition).

G119. **U.S CONGRESS. HOUSE. COMMITTEE ON BANKING, FINANCE AND URBAN AFFAIRS. SUBCOMMITTEE ON FINANCIAL INSTITUTIONS SUPERVISION, REGULATION AND INSURANCE.**

Examine Japanese financial system and its affect on ability of U.S. firms to compete. Hearing before the Subcommittee on Financial Institutions Supervision, Regulation and Insurance (and) Task Force on International Competitiveness of U.S. Financial Institutions of the Committee on Banking, Finance and Urban Affairs, House of Representatives, 101st Congress, 2nd session. Aug. 2, 1990, Washington, G.P.O., 1990, p. 145. Serial no. 101–162.

G120. **U.S. CONGRESS. JOINT ECONOMIC COMMITTEE.**

The international adjustment process. Hearing, 101st Congress, 1st session. Sept. 27, 1990, Washington, G.P.O., 1989, p. 71. (Hearing, Senate, 101st Congress, 1st session, S. Hrg. 101–751) reviews the question of the current account and trade imbalances in the world economy....In the last year, for the first time in 30 years, the United States had begun to report deficits in trade and services, particularly for investment earnings. This reflects rising payments to foreigners on their assets.

G121. **U.S. GENERAL ACCOUNTING OFFICE.**

Export promotion: U.S. Government promotional activities in Japan; briefing report to the Honorable Les AuCoin, House of Representatives. Feb. 21, 1989, Washington, G.A.O., 1989, p. 13. Investigates staffing levels and quality of service provided by the U.S. and Foreign Commercial Service in promoting U.S. business interests in Japan. Includes views of U.S. businesses on the quality of assistance they received and discusses Japan's export promotion presence in the U.S. through the Japan External Trade Relations Organization (JETRO).

G122. **U.S. GENERAL ACCOUNTING OFFICE.**

Foreign investment: aspects of the U.S.–Japan relationship; fact sheet for the chairman, Committee on Commerce, Science, and Transportation, U.S. Senate. July 31, 1990. Washington, G.A.O., 1990, p. 20. Provides information on (1) the extent and sectoral composition of Japanese investment in the

United States and U.S. investment in Japan, (2) the forms of Japanese direct investment in the United States, and (3) barriers to U.S. investment in Japan.

G123. **U.S. GENERAL ACCOUNTING OFFICE.**
International trade: revitalizing the U.S. machine tool industry; report to the Honorable Helen Delich Bentley, House of Representatives. July 17, 1990, Washington, G.A.O., 1990, p. 43. In December 1986, the United States concluded 5-year voluntary restraint agreements with Japan and Taiwan to limit their exports in certain categories of machine tools. At the same time, the United States requested that nine other countries limit their U.S. machine tool market shares to specific amounts or to 1986 levels. These latter requests were made to help ensure that domestic manufacturing rather than foreign competitors would be able to take advantage of the reduction in Japan's and Taiwan's market shares.

G124. **U.S. INTERNATIONAL TRADE ADMINISTRATION. OFFICE OF FOREST PRODUCTS AND DOMESTIC CONSTRUCTION. BASIC INDUSTRIES SECTOR.**
The Japanese solid wood products market: profile and outlook. The Washington Administration, 1989, p. 194. Contents—Executive summary. Impediments to increased solid wood products exports to Japan. Japanese consumption of forest products. Japan's forest resources. Japan's wood based industries. Barriers to trade. International trade.

G125. Yoshitomi, M. **KEIRETSU: AN INSIDER'S GUIDE TO JAPAN'S CONGLOMERATES.** *International Economic Insights*, Vol. 1, Sept.–Oct. 1990, pp. 10–17.
Describes the main features of Japan's large conglomerate organizations ("Keiretsu") in the areas of production, finance, and distribution. Concludes that it is too early to say whether the Japanese economic system, characterized by keiretsu, will prove to be one of the legitimate and viable capitalist systems and therefore a model for other countries. Includes article by Chalmers Johnson (Keiretsu: an outsider's view).

G126. Yoshitomi, M. **YEN APPRECIATION, STRUCTURAL REFORMS AND EXTERNAL IMBALANCES—INTERNATIONAL AND DOMESTIC FACTORS IN JAPAN'S ECONOMIC ADJUSTMENT.** *International Spectator*, Vol. 24, July–Dec. 1989, pp. 198–207.
Examines structural change and reform in Japan following the rapid appreciation in the yen and the rapid growth rate of the Japanese economy since 1987. Claims that liberalization has occurred in agriculture, air transportation, and the distribution system. By contrast, land and urban development policies have been slow in deregulating.

G127. Zen'ichi, S. **A TEXAN RAID ON A JAPANESE COMPANY.** *Japan Echo*, Vol. 16, Winter 1990, pp. 61–66.
Considers the problem sin investment relations between Japan and the U.S. in light of T. Boon Pickens' attempt to gain representation on the board of Koito Manufacturing Co. The incident represents a clash between the shareholders first culture of American business and the Japanese approach, which gives precedence to the interests of employees.

G128. Zhang, D. and Kuroda, K. **BEWARE OF JAPANESE NEGOTIATION STYLE: HOW TO NEGOTIATE WITH JAPANESE COMPANIES.** *Northwestern Journal of International Law and Business*, Vol. 10, Fall 1989, pp. 195–212.

Article discusses traditional Japanese concepts of order, hierarchy, seniority, and social harmony, which in turn have formed the unique Japanese negotiation styles of step-by-step negotiation and consensus decision-making or the ringi system. With the expansion of Japanese business activities into the international arena, however, Japanese negotiations may adjust their tactics to achieve their objectives.

G129. Zielinski, R. and Holloway, N. **UNEQUAL EQUITIES: POWER AND RISK IN JAPAN'S STOCKMARKET**. Kodansha International, 246 pp.

SUBJECT INDEX

AUTHOR INDEX

ISBN 1-56072-049